BFI Modern Class

C000152214

**Rob White**
Series Editor

Advancing into its second century, the cinema is now a mature art form with an established list of classics. But contemporary cinema is so subject to every shift in fashion regarding aesthetics, morals and ideas that judgments on the true worth of recent films are liable to be risky and controversial; yet they are essential if we want to know where the cinema is going and what it can achieve.

As part of the British Film Institute's commitment to the promotion and evaluation of contemporary cinema, and in conjunction with the influential BFI Film Classics series, BFI Modern Classics is a series of books devoted to individual films of recent years. Distinguished film critics, scholars and novelists explore the production and reception of their chosen films in the context of an argument about the film's importance. Insightful, considered, often impassioned, these elegant, beautifully illustrated books will set the agenda for debates about what matters in modern cinema.

# Independence Day, or How I Learned to Stop Worrying and Love the Enola Gay

**Michael Rogin**

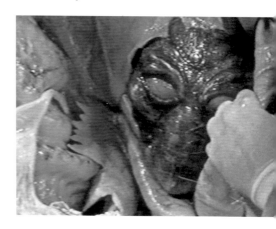

 Publishing

First published in 1998 by the
**British Film Institute**
21 Stephen Street, London W1P 2LN

Copyright © Michael Rogin 1998

The British Film Institute is the UK national
agency with responsibility for encouraging
the arts of film and television and conserving
them in the national interest.

Series design by Andrew Barron &
Collis Clements Associates

Typeset in Italian Garamond
by D R Bungay Associates, Burghfield, Berks

Picture editing by Millie Simpson

Designed by Tom Cabot and Rob White

Printed in Great Britain by
Norwich Colour Print, Drayton, Norfolk

British Library Cataloguing-in-Publication Data
A catalogue record for this book is available
from the British Library
ISBN 0-85170-662-2

# Contents

To Gastón and Alyson for this book, and to my other Berkeley
students, present and past.

## Acknowledgments

Thanks to Gastón Alonso-Donate and Alyson Cole for the good material and good ideas; to Kathy Moran, Lon Troyer, Kim Chernin, Richard Hutson, Shannon Stimson, Paul Thomas, Marcus Williamsen, Carol Clover, Ann Banfield, and participants at the Humanities Center, Johns Hopkins, and Ruth Mayer's workshop at the Englisches Seminar, Universität zu Köln, for their comments on earlier versions of this essay; to Rob White of the British Film Institute for his excellent advice and help with sources; to Carolyn Russo for photos of the Enola Gay,  and Millie Simpson for picture editing; and to the members of my seminar on 'The Body and the Body Politic', Fall 1996, with whom I first watched and discussed *Independence Day*.

I've often wondered, what if all of us in the world discovered that we were threatened by an outer – a power from outer space, from another planet. Wouldn't we all of a sudden find that we didn't have any differences between us at all, we were all human beings, citizens of the world, and wouldn't we come together to fight that particular threat?

President Ronald Reagan, May 8, 1988. Terence Hunt (AP White House Correspondent), 'Reagan-Space Invaders', Associated Press dispatch, 9 May, 1988.

# 1 Film as Politics

*Independence Day*, the first election-year motion picture to receive the
endorsement of both major party Presidential candidates, opened to
national acclaim on 2 July 1996, the day that alien spacecraft were first
sighted. 'I recommend it,' President Bill Clinton told a crowd the next
morning. Hillary, Bill and Chelsea Clinton watched the incineration of
the White House on 2 July from the scene of the crime. They were
joined by Dean Devlin and Roland Emmerich, who produced, directed
and wrote the film, and by the film Chief Executive, Bill Pullman, who
sat next to his real-life counterpart. President Clinton comforted his
daughter when she took fright at the obliteration of her home; soon
after, the on-screen President would comfort his daughter when her
mother, who had been away from the White House on business, died
from the effects of the blast that levelled Los Angeles.[1]

Hollywood and Washington, twin capitals of the American empire
and seats of its international political economy, collaborated to promote
the movie that filmed their destruction. Cementing the alliance between
entertainment and aerospace as the top two American export industries
(the former had just passed the latter to move into first place),
*Independence Day* had been filmed with full military co-operation.[2] The
Fox production, to be sure, was hardly the first film shown at the White
House; that honour belongs to *The Birth of a Nation*. Franklin and
Eleanor Roosevelt had screened *Gone with the Wind*, Nixon watched
*Patton*, and among the old movies that entertained Ronald and Nancy
Reagan every night were several starring the Chief Executive. Not since
the House UnAmerican Activities Committee investigated Communist
influence in motion pictures at the onset of the Cold War, however, had
Hollywood become a major bone of contention in two-party politics. Bob
Dole had energised his run for the Republican nomination in 1995 by
condemning the 'nightmares of depravity', the 'casual violence and more
casual sex' in motion pictures. 'We have reached the point where our
popular culture threatens to undermine our character as a nation,' Dole
had warned. Now, seeking a *rapprochement* with the entertainment

business and looking for positive alternatives to such films as *Natural Born Killers* and *Strip Tease*, the Presidential candidate endorsed a movie in which an alien invasion wipes out roughly a hundred million humans before an American-led, 4 July victory.[3]

Imitating his family-values Presidential opponent, Dole celebrated his wife's sixtieth birthday at a southern California matinee of the film. The Doles were accompanied by Ken Khachigian, chair of the California Republican Presidential campaign, and by William Bennett, former Education Secretary, former Director of the Office of National Drug Control Policy, and author of a best-selling collection of uplifting tales, *The Book of Virtues*. Bennett, believing that Hollywood has inherited the institutional moral power once held by the medieval Catholic Church, had urged Dole to see this example of the motion picture industry's capacity to do good. Although Bennett objects to government overregulation of corporations which pollute the environment, there is one crusade against 'toxic waste' that wins his full endorsement, Wal-Mart's censorship of sex-and-violence lyrics from the CDs sold in its stores. Instead of tolerating 'gangsta rap', in Bennett's view, parents should bring their children to watch a hundred million asexual and uncasual deaths.[4]

Deprived of Clinton's access to the White House, Dole issued his own endorsement of *Independence Day* from Fox's padded sound stage.

Fox is part of the media empire of the recently naturalised Australian alien, Rupert Murdoch, himself a major contributor to the Dole campaign. Murdoch's Fox and Star TV networks reported the alien invasion within the Fox production, thereby advertising themselves as well. Although *Independence Day* aggrandised Murdoch and Fox, Dole's plug aided neither his campaign, which needed the help, nor the film, which did not. The Republican Presidential candidate seemed to be the last person in America to see *Independence Day*, which had benefited from unprecedented media attention in the weeks before it opened. 'Probably the most successful trailer in movie history' blew up the White House over and over again in cineplexes around the country. Fox culminated its highly-praised advance advertising campaign on 2 July with newspaper ads promising that 'the question of whether or not we are alone in the universe will be answered tonight'. *Time* and *Newsweek* ran cover stories to coincide with the movie's release.[5]

Opening day enthusiasm ranged from mass to elite opinion. Of the top ten grossing motion pictures of 1996, *Independence Day* received by far the highest positive (66.7%) and lowest negative (4.7%) percentage of reviews. Janet Maslin in the *New York Times* thrilled at the 'rush of gleeful, audience-friendly exhilaration'. 'Anyone appalled that movie audiences can enjoy such widespread catastrophe can be assured that

"Independence Day" is really about togetherness and catharsis,' wrote Maslin, for, although 'the planet sure is in peril', the movie-makers 'keep the crisis seeming mercifully benign'. The movie did commit one transgression, according to Maslin, not in its casual attitude toward mass destruction but in Judd Hirsch's 'regrettable ethnic stereotype' of a

Aliens incinerate the White House

'pesky Jewish father'. We will return to the significance of this overkill, for Maslin hardly wanted Jews to boycott a movie whose heroic triumvirate included the father's Jewish son. Spurred by the advance publicity, the *Time* and *Newsweek* cover stories, and the Presidential and *New York Times* endorsements, *Independence Day* opened to the most successful week in the entire history of motion pictures. It ended the year as the top-grossing movie of 1996 in the United States, the United Kingdom, Germany and around the world, becoming the sixth top domestic-grosser of all time.[6]

'I liked it,' Dole reported when he finally caught up with President Clinton and the American people and went to see the film. The candidate placed *Independence Day* with *Forrest Gump* (the top grosser and top Academy Award winner of 1994, and third top-grossing film of all time) as movies which did not 'deride our country and our values'. 'We won in the end,' Dole explained. 'Bring your family too. You'll be proud of it. Diversity. America. Leadership. Good over Evil.'[7]

'They struck us in the middle of the night, those sneaks. We are good, they are bad. Let's all get together we said, and we creamed them. We started from way behind. We found strength in this common commitment, this commonality, community, family. … You never had a war quite like that.' Even to the telegraphic syntax, Dole's endorsement uncannily echoed the words of former New York governor Mario Cuomo a year earlier. But whereas Clinton and Dole were looking forward to 'togetherness and catharsis' in the interplanetary wartime future, Cuomo was nostalgic for the past. 'The idea of coming together was best served in my lifetime in the Second World War,' Cuomo explained on the fiftieth anniversary of VE Day. His wish to, in his word, 're-create' World War II was fulfilled through the magic of *ID4*; I for Independence, D for Day, 4 for 4 July. *ID4*, the advertised code name for *Independence Day*, invoked the innovative computer graphics so heavily attended to in the advance publicity for the film. Joining American national rebirth to the computer revolution, *ID4*'s digital interventions on and off camera repelled an alien invasion without any planes actually leaving the ground.[8]

Quintessential 'nineteen Hollywood cinema', *Independence Day* has been seen 'as a smart, ironic, interweaving of codes that appeal to the culturally hyperconscious viewer', a self-referential set of special effects constituted by the ingestion of other films. 'The social relevance of *Independence Day* is that it scarely has any,' explains Caryn James. From this perspective *Independence Day* takes its place as the most successful among the recent crop of blockbusters made for an audience of teenage boys, films that 'want, in the worst way, to say nothing'. To find meaning in such a movie is to risk becoming one with those other out-of-touch old fogies, William Bennett and Bob Dole, the exposed negative to their positive thinking. That is particularly the case for cinephiles of classic Hollywood and European art cinema, who have kept their disapproving distance from science fiction and the other genres of the New Hollywood. But perhaps the cultural illiteracy of these viewers (think of them as the proverbial visitors from Mars) will defamiliarise the current common sense shared between Hollywood and Washington. Risking self-exposure, then, I will propose the alternative to the say-nothing hypothesis, that *Independence Day* wants in the worst way to say something, and that it does so by morphing into entertainment fantasy the two exterminatory culminations of World War II, one from the European and the other from the Asian theatre. In the name of multiculturalism but against its actual contemporary exemplars, and with Jew, black and public-spirited WASP as its front men, *ID4* re-fights World War II as virtual reality. Bringing up to date the Cold War liberal, military, post-industrial, enfotainment complex, and using bodily invasion to electrify the body politic, *Independence Day* is the defining motion picture of Bill Clinton's America.[9]

## **2** History as Film

World War II was certainly on the minds both of those who saw and of those who made *Independence Day*. The co-operation between WASP President from Washington, black pilot from Los Angeles and Jewish computer genius from New York, that wipes out the alien menace, reminded *New York* magazine film critic David Denby of Hollywood's World War II multi-ethnic platoons. *Independence Day* was 'like a patriotic World War II movie rarely made anymore', according to the *New York Times*, and that accounted for its popularity. Bill Pullman 'got to play the kind of lead I can remember William Holden playing in those old World War II pictures'. Dole compared *Independence Day* to *Schindler's List*. Like the holocaust film, explained a campaign spokesman, *Independence Day* 'preserves the notion of patriotism, mankind coming together and the fight between good and evil'. The violence is 'socially redeeming' in both films, Dole's spokesman continued, 'essential to the plot, and promotes a greater good'. Along with the end of the Cold War, political correctness was said to have ruled

William Holden in *The Devil's Brigade* (1968)

out an entire century of movie villains – Indians, Latinos, African-Americans, Russians. 'It's politically incorrect to use any nationality for bad guys,' explained Emmerich. Hence 'Aliens are the best movie villains since Nazis.'[10]

Emmerich and Devlin, one German and the other American, immediately locate their film in the ambience of World War II. Instantly recognisable patriotic icons – Statue of Liberty, Lincoln Memorial, Washington Monument – flash on screen in the opening minutes of the film. The first of these, and the only scene of war, is the statue of American soldiers raising the flag on Iwo Jima. When the pilot leading the first assault on the alien invasion issues his 'lock 'n' load' command, the reference goes back through Pat Buchanan's 1996 Presidential campaign slogan to the original source, John Wayne's classic *Sands of Iwo Jima*.[11] Although that first attack fails, the American military employs 'the old Morse Code' at the film's climax to (a double World War II invocation) inform Sahara British and Arabs how to penetrate the enemy's defence.

*Independence Day* entered production at the peak of World War II nostalgia, during the year marking the fiftieth anniversary of the end of the war. Doris Kearns Goodwin won the Pulitzer prize in 1995 for *No Ordinary Time*, her best-selling evocation of the White House and the country at war. The Republican Party ran World War II veterans for President in the elections of 1988, 1992 and 1996, a progression that was looking increasingly parodic during the run-up to *Independence Day*. Although nostalgia is often a flight from current intractable problems, World War II nostalgists were deliberately putting the recovery of the past to contemporary political use. Like Cuomo and Dole, Kearns Goodwin drew lessons for the present from the national unity and higher purpose of America at war.[12]

*ID4*'s return to World War II offers a multicultural reuniting of America on violently exclusionary terms. But before turning to the film's contribution to the contemporary diversity debate, we must first attend to the past. Nostalgia creates imaginary ideal objects to flee old as well as present-day troubles, and simulating 'World War II' as happy substitute for the actual war confronted the problem of past horror in a particularly virulent form. There was no way to bring back World War II without calling up its massive, unprecedented, exterminatory violence. Although hardly exhausting that slaughter, two names have come to encapsulate it, Holocaust and Hiroshima: each evidences the splitting required to preserve an ideal object, but in opposed ways. The Holocaust against the Jews, with some re-writing of history, thematises the split between good and evil as the *raison d'être* of 'the good war'. The atomic holocaust, by joining moral ambiguity to mass destruction, was challenging World War II nostalgia at its core.

In *Schindler's List*, the massive critical, popular and Academy Award success of 1993, World War II nostalgia issued forth in a feel-good Holocaust film;[13] the atmospherics and Jewish hero of *Independence Day*, to which we will return, are a residue from the Spielberg production. But thanks to a major public controversy over the commemoration of the end of the war, *Independence Day* had also to ingest that other holocaust, Hiroshima.

The Smithsonian Museum, keeper of American historical memory, planned its exhibit to commemorate the allied victory around the plane that dropped the first atomic bomb, the Enola Gay. But instead of treating the atomic explosion as triumphalist ending to World War – 'one of the most morally unambiguous events of the twentieth century', as seven congressmen would soon put it – the Smithsonian National Air Museum proposed to feature the Enola Gay as the horrifying beginning of the atomic age. This revisionism took two forms. First, the exhibit would challenge the politically sacred belief that the bombs dropped on Hiroshima and Nagasaki saved more lives than they destroyed. Relying on contemporary scholarship and on actual estimates at the time, the original script drastically reduced what had become the magic number of American casualties – an unchallenged fact when I was growing up – that would have resulted from an invasion of Japan, and allowed debate as to whether the bombs had even been necessary to forestall an invasion and force Japanese surrender. Second, curators planned to display the results at ground zero, the impact on human bodies and artefacts of the birth of the atom bomb. This unprecedented, instantaneous mass destruction from a single weapon, with its horrifying visible and invisible permanent after-effects, was now to receive officially-sanctioned public display. The 'images of atrocity and slaughter', as the script called them, would be followed by a coda invoking a 'World Gone M.A.D.' (the acronym for American nuclear deterrence strategy, Mutual Assured Destruction), a world of 'nuclear waste and human experiments', 'nuclear proliferation and nuclear terrorism'.[14]

The original 1945 American responses to Hiroshima and Nagasaki had mixed celebration with what one widely-quoted writer labelled 'primordial apprehensions'. *Time* called the end of the war 'the most grimly Pyrrhic of victories'. Dismembered and stored away after its flight, the Enola Gay had never been awarded public iconic status, and although one politician compared the plane's disappearance to 'mothballing the Statue of Liberty or the first space capsule that landed on the moon' (both would appear in *Independence Day*), its invisibility had the virtue of sending underground the initial atomic anxieties. Now with stunning innocence about the politics and psychopathology of history, the planners of the Enola Gay exhibit were forcing Americans to attend to the fact that the successful conclusion of World War II in the birth of the atomic age marked what Tom Engelhardt has called 'the end of victory culture'.[15]

Hiroshima had introduced, to be sure, a half-century nuclear balance of terror rather than another big bang, and the Cold War stalemate had itself come recently to a triumphal end with the fall of another 'empire of evil'. But it was that failure of Cold War victory to breathe new life into the United States that had intensified World War II nostalgia in the first place. From this perspective, then, the ideal America lay back across the great divide opened up by Hiroshima, and World War II was on the far side. The proposed Enola Gay exhibit memorialised a break with the past: a new, apocalyptic, paralysing beginning.

From another perspective, however, which was also finding its way into official commemorations, the end of World War II was disturbing because of its historical continuity. Air power provided the most direct link between Hiroshima and the history of the United States. The National Air and Space Museum had functioned from its inception as a wing of the aerospace industry, patriotically celebrating airborne technological might. However, its recent 'Great War in the Air' exhibit, as one historian put it, 'massively debunks the "Hollywood" romanticisation of pilots and planes in World War I ... [and] concludes with a video that conveys, in terse, shocking footage, the horrendously destructive legacy of strategic bombing that followed World War I – from World War II through the US air war against Indochina to the high-tech

Urban destruction

air strikes by Americans in the Gulf War of 1991'. The video pictured what Winston Churchill – he of 'the old Morse code' – had christened 'terror bombing', the incinerations of Dresden and Tokyo. An aide to General Douglas MacArthur called the saturation bombing of Japan that preceded Hiroshima 'one of the most ruthless and barbaric killings of noncombatants in all history'. Well before Hiroshima and Nagasaki, writes John Dower, 'combatants on all sides had identified civilian populations as legitimate and indeed primary targets'. 'The very concept of strategic bombing', the photojournal *Life* declared in 1945, 'led

straight to Hiroshima.' From this vantage point Hiroshima and Nagasaki looked less like radical departures than incremental next steps. It was as if the Air and Space Museum were daring Hollywood to make its own 'Great War in the Air', a film that would redeem American history as historians no longer seemed able to do.[16]

*Independence Day* is that film, with the weapons of American victory first put into alien hands. Just as the only precedents for using the alien's 'primary weapon' are Hiroshima and Nagasaki, so the firestorms that incinerate the Empire State Building and the White House, and lay waste to Los Angeles, New York and Washington, DC, resemble nothing so much as the incendiary effects of American air power from World War II to Vietnam – unless it be the imaginings of World War III produced in the wake of Hiroshima. 'Every major city will be wiped out in thirty minutes,' forecast the editor of *Astounding Science Fiction* in August 1945. 'New York will be a slag heap.' Closer yet to *Independence Day* was 'The 36-Hour War' imagined by the Commander of the Army Air Force in November 1945 and illustrated by a cover story in *Life*. An unnamed 'enemy of the United States' drops missiles on thirteen American cities before the United States fights back and wins.[17]

Air power from its inception was the new frontier that would compensate for the end of the old one, and the end of victory culture cast its shadow over old frontier triumphs as well. In its 1991 installation, 'The West in America: Reinterpreting Images of the Frontier, 1820–1920', the Smithsonian had presented the march west from the perspective of the land and peoples that stood in the way. From that vantage point World War II culminated frontier history domestically in the incarceration of west-coast Japanese-Americans. The National Museum of American History's 1987 exhibit commemorating those camps still remains in place. Finally, as if to sum up all the assaults on the inherited history of the United States, a national commission of teachers of history had proposed new standards mandating what students should learn about the American past: more bottom-up social and less top-down political history, more named and anonymous women and peoples of colour, and less heroic dead white men.[18]

(Photo by
A. Leydenfrost;
copyright proprietor
unknown)

THE 36-HOUR WAR BEGINS WITH THE ATOMIC BOMBARDMENT OF KEY U.S. CITIES. HERE A SHOWER OF WHITE-HOT ENEMY ROCKETS FALLS ON WASHINGTON, D.C.

# THE 36-HOUR WAR

ARNOLD REPORT HINTS AT THE CATASTROPHE OF THE NEXT GREAT CONFLICT

These revisions of sacred collective memory came under increasing, widely-publicised, attack. Condemned in Congress and the mass media, 'Reinterpreting Images of the Frontier' was modified and itself prevented from travelling west. The United States Senate voted 99–1 that the *National Standards for United States History* not be certified by the federal government, and that funds to establish future standards go only to those with 'a decent respect for the contributions of Western civilization, and United States history'.[19] Under aerospace and congressional pressure, the Smithsonian director cancelled the original Enola Gay show. The curators and historians accused of political correctness were actually its victims, however, since their challenges to political correctness had mobilised the interested keepers of American memory. A chasm had opened between historical awareness and false memory syndrome, between the buried past that professionals were uncovering and

(Overleaf) The Enola Gay restored (photo by Carolyn Russo; by permission of Carolyn Russo and the National Air and Space Museum)

imaginary histories of the United States. Out of that chasm would emerge a product of those whose profession is the imaginary, the makers of *Independence Day*.

Like any symptom, the charge of political correctness exposed the truth as it distorted it, for the recovery of a more accurate American history itself had political origins. It emerged from the largest shock to American collective self-regard since the Great Depression, the conjunction of the mass movement against white supremacy at home with the war in Vietnam. This double crisis culminated in mass domestic social disorder, American military defeat, a failed executive coup, and the only Presidential and Vice-Presidential resignations in American history. It ushered in a new political regime dominated by the power of money, whose public face is race and multicultural conflict, in which the military-industrial complex has lost the (World War II grounded) ideological halo that once sacralised our political economy. Although Democrats retained control of Congress until 1994, the Republican Party seemed to have a lock on the White House. The only re-elected Democratic President since FDR, Clinton came to power in a period of conservative hegemony that began electorally with Richard Nixon's first victory, in reaction to the Vietnam War and racial and student protest, and (interrupted by Watergate) decisively took control of public policy under the second President from southern California (Nixon was the first), Ronald Reagan. Clinton is bringing the Democratic Party into the new political order, and *Independence Day* will help us see how.

Vietnam, Iran-Contra and the Gulf War all failed to do the work of World War II, and each registers within *Independence Day*: the alchoholic Vietnam veteran pilot suffers from post-traumatic stress disorder, the Defense Secretary invokes Oliver North and John Poindexter's 'plausible deniability' to justify keeping the original alien landing secret from the President (Poindexter, Reagan's National Security Adviser, was claiming to have protected his Chief Executive from knowledge of the link between two of Reagan's own pet projects, trading hostages for illegal arms shipments to Iran, with the profits financing illegal aid to the Nicaraguan contras), and the President cannot transfer his Gulf War

heroism to the White House. ('They elected a warrior and they got a wimp'.) The stage is set for redemptive World War.

In record-breaking popularity, message and the use of special effects, *Independence Day* is the successor to *Forrest Gump*. The two films approach their common project in apparently opposite ways: one through stitching documentary and staged historical footage into a local odyssey of unselfconscious individual virtue; the other through tongue-in-cheek intergalactic warfare, so that whereas *Forrest Gump* won six academy awards, *ID4* scored only for special effects. The former film brings its simple private hero, unchanged and untouched, through American historical violence, which opens with the Ku Klux Klan (since Forrest was named for KKK founder Nathan Bedford Forrest), and extends through Vietnam, political assassination and the Black Panthers. The latter film invents a gargantuan crisis that, dwarfing any actual historical catastrophe, re-animates the public world through violence.

However, both movies manifest an unremarked upon feature that has entered the New Hollywood in their attention to political concerns. Thematically the films share their large timely subjects – war, redemption through interracial friendship and (*ID4*'s subtext, as we shall see) AIDS.

*Forrest Gump*

They share as well the formal breakdown of the distinction between history and film. Forrest, a creature of both whose inability to tell the difference between them speaks for the movie, narrates his own birth as *Birth of a Nation* footage puts the Klan on screen. As the first newsreel in *Forrest Gump*, followed by Forrest digitally inserted next to John F. Kennedy, Lyndon Johnson and Richard Nixon, *Birth* prepares the way for *Independence Day* as docudrama. Incorporating American history in the service of American innocence, *Forrest Gump* and *Independence Day* enter the gap between what the keepers of American tradition want to believe and the history that has been forced on their attention.

Opponents of revisionist accounts of the American past can no longer supply credible narratives to replace the ones they label unpatriotic. So the Air and Space Museum finally exhibited the restored forward fuselage of the Enola Gay alone, incorporated into no narrative at all. What was left behind, writes Tom Engelhardt, was only the object itself, about which no story could any longer be told. At least not by historians. Where history fails, science fiction steps in, projecting into the future the terms on which the United States can redemptively recover its past. Avoiding all controversy, the Air and Space Museum called its next big show 'Star Wars'. Celebrating the twentieth anniversary of the original release of the film, it opened as *Star Wars* was appearing in motion picture theatres once again.[20]

## 3 Science as Fiction

*Independence Day* is not the first Hollywood blockbuster that (to invert the plot of another film of this period, *Back to the Future*), goes forward in order to go backward. That honour belongs to *Star Wars*, itself set 'a long time ago', the movie that made science fiction commercially viable and is now thanks to its (*Independence Day* stimulated) re-release the top-grossing film of all time. After a decade in which Hollywood registered the twin crises over race and Vietnam with (however one values them in retrospect) the most corrosive films about the United States ever to emerge from the dream factory, it began to produce what Robin Wood has called children's films for adults. Motion pictures like *Bonnie and Clyde*, *Easy Rider*, *Medium Cool*, *Nashville* and *Taxi Driver* registered American disintegration thematically and formally on screen. The decade running symbolically from the assassination of Kennedy to the resignation of Nixon recalls earlier periods of social upheaval in the United States – the 1860s, 1886–96, the 1930s – but it is entirely unprecedented in Hollywood history. When the New Hollywood reinstituted the power of positive thinking, incorporating catastrophes and triumphing over them, it had to do so on a new scale. Responding to the shattering of the reality effect as credible, reassuring, historical narrative – on the streets and on the screen – the New Hollywood produced comic book versions of epic conflicts on earth and in outer space that shattered box office records.[21]

Blockbuster driven, the New Hollywood 'went into high gear' in 1975 with *Jaws*, the first of the new record-setting films. The mid-1970s, writes Tom Schatz, initiated 'the first period of sustained economic vitality and industry stability since the classical period'. Earlier in the decade Hollywood had featured the disaster films that Emmerich and Devlin wanted to re-create in *Independence Day*. Lacking combat adventure and extraterrestrial appeal, however, and infiltrated by the absent presence of the political disasters surrounding them, disaster films never achieved the popularity of *ID4*'s other generic precedent, science fiction. With the *Star Wars* and *Indiana Jones* trilogies and *E.T.*, the New

Hollywood came into its own. In their 'combination of narrative conservatism and technical wizardry', as Scott Bukatman points out, New Hollywood blockbusters hark back to such Disney animated features as *Snow White* (1937), *Fantasia* (1940), *Bambi* (1942) and *Cinderella* (1949), the only films made before the 1950s, *Gone with the Wind* aside, that, adjusting for inflation and ticket price rises, remain among the top twenty domestic box office attractions.[22]

New Hollywood founders George Lucas and Steven Spielberg may not have been Ronald Reagan's political supporters, but they anticipated and participated in the Reagan counter-revolution. The visual media swallowed up history in the Hollywood–Washington Reagan regime, presided over by the former actor who capitalised on his confusion of film with the world outside it. Star Wars encapsulates the new order, with Reagan borrowing the idea for the super defensive weapon from one of his own World War II movies, *Murder in the Air*, and its name from the Lucas science fiction.[23]

Emmerich and Devlin, born 1955 and 1962, belong to a younger generation of film-makers than the New Hollywood founders. Coming of age after the battle, they comfortably inhabit the closed world of visual self-referentiality, exploiting New Hollywood special effects without creating the rupturing impact of the original films. *Independence Day*, Clinton's movie, routinises the Reagan–Lucas charisma. As Devlin 'confesses', 'For me the movies of George Lucas and Steven Spielberg are still the greatest movies ever.' Speaking of *Independence Day*, he adds 'We didn't want to try and hide the fact that this film could not exist without *War of the Worlds*, without *The Day the Earth Stood Still*, without *Star Wars* or *Close Encounters*,' since those films are 'part of our "collective unconscious"'.[24]

New Hollywood blockbusters follow the cartoon features in multiplying box office receipts, as families that come together into motion picture theatres augment repeat attendance by children and teenagers. Thanks to audience expansion, the popularity of these record-setting films is not strictly comparable to that of mature entertainments. The New Hollywood's organisation around motion pictures that cross over from adolescent to adult audiences is none the less all the more worthy of attention.

How to understand *ID4*'s conflation of political and Hollywood history, of the message that won the endorsement of political elites and the medium of film self-referentiality? Kathleen Moran has suggested a distinction between 'made for' and 'made by', between the teenage boys targeted by special effects films and the baby boomers who created the New Hollywood (and who constitute much of its audience as well).[25] For those born in the wake of World War II who lived through the 1960s upheavals, like the baby boomer in the White House, *Independence Day* promises the restoration of victory culture; it speaks to the disturbances of history with which I began. For culturally literate teenage boys, by contrast, the relevant history is only the history of film. Generationally between the two groups, Devlin and Emmerich locate their 'collective unconscious' entirely within movies. The collectively unconscious extrafilmic world returns, however, not only in explicit political intrafilm references but also in the new motion picture syntax. For New Hollywood special effects do not simply carry us off to faraway worlds or bring them close to home. Making sensate the visual and stimulating visceral adolescent excitement, special effects also focus on the vulnerable human body. The graphic body parts close-ups of torture and other forms of violence, from the *Rambo* and *Terminator* films to *Pulp Fiction*, are of particular interest to young men. Just as among older viewers virtual visual reality stands for the historical body politic, for young and mature alike, *Independence Day* is one of any number of films to address the subjects I will turn to later in this text: bodily desire, illness and anxiety. Self-awareness does not dull sensation, any more in the New Hollywood than in the primitive cinema of attractions (early sensation films less interested in story than in the new medium's power to shock), thanks to the somatising impact of jump cuts, speeded-up motion and other special effects. The genre conventions and interfilmic quotations that insulate viewers from troubling public and private material inhibit psychic censorship and propel disturbance to the surface of the spectacle. Politicians and attentive publics in the aftermath of the

Cold War worry about the discrediting of American history and the disuniting of America. For male adolescents, and not only for them, orifices and vulnerable bodily borders are the locus of anxiety.[26]

Playful with body parts small and writ large, the Freudian repressed now entirely on the surface, Devlin and Emmerich consciously mobilise film's 'collective unconscious' to make a political movie. Having established the power of motion pictures to overwhelm history by moving under water, back in time and out in space, New Hollywood film-makers can now return to the political world – in films like *Schindler's List*, *Forrest Gump* and *Independence Day* – exercising the authority of film. But Emmerich and Devlin are not entirely in control of the ways in which the history of the body politic has entered their movie, exposing a more disturbing political unconscious than their patriotic celebration intends.[27] Exposing it to few opinion leaders or members of the mass public, however, as the conjunction of the body and the body politic organised *ID4*, propelled it to its climax, and brought America, however fleetingly, together.

The birth of the atomic age had itself broken down the distinction between grownups and children. Hiroshima and Nagasaki produced

*Rambo: First Blood, Part II*

atomic war games at penny arcades. As one observer put it in 1948, where once 'you could try your luck shooting at a helpless parachutist as he drifted toward the ground, you can now try your luck at wiping out a whole city with an atomic bomb'. 'We are like children playing with a concentrated instrument of death whose destructive potential our little minds cannot grasp,' warned the radio voice of H.V. Kaltenborn. The 1950s 'age of anxiety' grasped that potential in science fiction films like *Invaders from Mars* and *War of the Worlds*. Such movies registered the doubled menace of atomic and Cold War destruction to which World War II had given birth. *War of the Worlds*, for example, begins with brief footage of war's airborne violence from World War I through the atomic bomb to the Martian attack, and ends with 'all that men could do [having] failed'. *Independence Day* cites *War of the Worlds*, as we shall see, to evacuate the anxiety of the original film; it reduces adults to children in the service of security, not terror. Like other contemporary disaster blockbusters, it revives that 1970s genre to 'enact the fantasy of conjuring up doomsday, yet controlling it'. But whereas disaster films like *Airport* were in their original incarnation transitional between the disintegrative cinema of the Johnson–Nixon years and anticipatory Reaganite reassurance, the contemporary product remains deliberately, calmingly, one-dimensional. The fate of the earth can hang in the balance in *ID4* because nothing is really at stake.[28]

Scientific technology restores the illusion of being in control at a double cost to the reality principle, however, and *Independence Day*'s Academy Award-winning confusion of the special effect with the real shows both costs on screen. *ID4* brings together two fallacies of misplaced concreteness, one as cyberspace virtual reality and the other as magical causal thinking. First, as ever more sophisticated special effects convincingly counterfeit reality, whether through the seamless mixture of documentary and fictional footage (as in *JFK* and *Forrest Gump*) or through models and computer-generated graphics (as in *ID4*), the simulacrum carries more conviction than any fragmentary, three-dimensional embodiment. There are more than 3,000 special effects shots in *Independence Day* and – another record – 120 shots using miniaturised models. Although 'the development of digital effects – the art of the impossible, immaterial image – has fuelled the return to prominence of science fiction', Jonathan Romney writes, it has at the same time enabled 'cinema … to heighten the sense of reality by expelling the real from its terms of reference'. The special effect's revived cinema of attractions substitutes aggressive, visually-coercive bodily stimulation for classical realism's observation of sense data, what Robert Bresson called the 'crude real recorded as it is by the camera'. As spectacle instantiates the present moment, in Leo Charney's analysis, so narrative – incorporating old films and allegorising history – makes present, as nostalgia, the past. The culturally literate mass public may know the difference between entertainment and life, but knowing disavowal of the former also deprives the latter of solid ground.[29]

Here the second defect of scientific power comes into play. Since few members of the mass public who consume the products of science can produce them, credulity plays a large role in the reception of scientifically-made counterfeits (as is testified to by the Sokal affair, in which a physicist passed off a parodic account of 'Quantum Gravity' on the cultural studies journal, *Social Text*, which published it as the real thing). Science offers materialist explanations of physical causality that only a small number of specialists (who vary from one discipline to another) can validate for themselves. Whereas some of the rest of us accept such explanations on faith, others turn to what Richard Lewontin has recently labelled 'demonological' causal understandings. Instead of trusting in a materialism whose invisibility to the naked eye violates common sense, scientific illiterates attribute causal power to hallucinated, physicalised, occult forces. Science wars have as a result entered contemporary politics alongside the history wars, in controversies over creationism, AIDS and extraterrestrial life. 'There are millions of Americans who probably know more about aliens than they do about thermodynamics,' reports one anthropologist. Half the American people – the statistic is cited both in Lewontin's article on popular resistance to science and in the *Newsweek* cover story on *Independence Day* – believe in the existence of Unidentified Flying Objects, piloted invaders from outer space. On 2 July 1996, thanks to the achievements of a science that refutes their existence in one universe as it makes them convincingly visible in another, these aliens entered American air space.[30]

Scientists, historians and aliens are not the only keepers of esoteric, secret knowledge; the top political and military figures that join them are featured in *Independence Day*. This juncture of power and knowledge, the military-industrial complex to which World War II and Hiroshima gave birth, has generated its own demonologies. Like the intertwined Communist and nuclear menaces that are visible in such Cold War science fictions as *Them!*[31] and *Invaders from Mars*, 'aliens' and 'thermodynamics' also turn out to have a family resemblance, since clandestine nuclear military activity has for half a century generated sightings of alien invaders outside of motion picture theatres as well as inside them.

The threat from an alien way of life, *Independence Day* knows, originated at our own nuclear home. Flying saucers were first spotted in the New Mexico desert in 1947, a time and place so close to Los Alamos and the Alamagordo atomic test-site as to suggest the atomic laboratory as their source. Area 51, Roswell, New Mexico, in the middle of atomic-alien territory, has long been the rumoured site of an alien landing. When a rancher brought some strange debris to the Roswell air force base in 1947, an air force spokesman initially reported a 'flying dish'. 'RAAF Captures Flying Saucer' headlined the 8 July *Roswell Daily Record*. The military quickly retracted the flying dish description, but UFO conventions have been living off Roswell for decades. Dean Devlin's actress mother dragged him in his childhood from one UFO convention to another. (One hopes she is not the model for the alien-welcoming exotic dancer incinerated in *ID4*.) 'Inside *Independence Day*', the Fox-produced CD-Rom on the making of the film, combines an account of *ID4*'s special effects with a 'History' section on flying saucers. Retired Air Force Lieutenant Colonel Wendelle Stevens, who evaluated captured Nazi weapons during World War II, appears in cyberspace to report the military capture of four live aliens after the Roswell crash. On the fiftieth anniversary of the 'flying dish', *Time* produced its second alien cover story in two years. Called *The Roswell Files*, the *Time* cover borrowed its

name from *The X Files*, the popular television series whose protagonists investigate extraterrestrial sightings. The news magazine predicted that the golden anniversary of the UFO landing, one year after the appearance of *ID4*, would draw 100,000 people to Roswell.[32]

Since the appearance of the Roswell flying saucer, Area 51 has been rumoured to house a secret military research installation investigating the alien presence. Exposing that research centre to the mass public, *ID4* gives it the name of a real agency, the Search for Extra-

(Top) *Roswell Daily Record*, front page, 8 July 1947 (by permission of the Roswell Daily Record)
(Bottom) Tiffany (Kiersten Warren) welcomes the aliens

The Search for
Extraterrestrial
Intelligence

terrestrial Intelligence Institute. Phillip Corso, a member of Eisenhower's
National Security Council, contended after the release of *Independence
Day* that he had directed an army project transferring the military
technology recovered from the alien ship that crashed at Roswell.
Extraterrestrials, claimed Corso, were the real targets of Reagan's
Strategic Defense Initiative, Star Wars. Thanks to the successful testing
of SDI, wrote the retired army intelligence officer, 'they knew we had our
defense of the planet in place.' (Corso was a former member of South
Carolina Senator Strom Thurmond's staff, and Thurmond initially
endorsed his book.)[33]

Half the American people believe a government plot has covered
up the existence of UFOs. The military finally acknowledged a cover-up
in the years surrounding *ID4*; the US government was hiding not aliens,
however, but its own covert Cold War activity. Rather than debris from
weather balloons, as the air force had long claimed, the Roswell flying
dish was what was left of an effort to monitor Soviet nuclear tests.
Strange-looking alien bodies, their existence denied for half a century,
were now said to be air force dummies dropped to test the results of
earth-impact at high altitudes. And the CIA now admitted that the air
force had made 'deceptive statements to the public' in attributing the
numerous UFO sightings in the 1950s and 1960s to atmospheric
conditions. The mysterious flying objects were actually high altitude
American spy planes heading for Soviet air space. Conspiracy theories
flourish 'when the lies come from above' (the headline over one story
reporting government mendacity); there are virtually the same number of
books in print on UFOs (256) as on the Kennedys (266).[34]

The President himself jocularly denied UFO rumours six months before *Independence Day* premiered. Comforting one child about political violence during a trip to Belfast, Bill Clinton reassured another, 'As far as I know, an alien spacecraft did not crash in Roswell, New Mexico in 1947. And, Ryan, if the United States Air Force did recover alien bodies, they didn't tell me about it either, and I want to know.' Bill Pullman, as *ID4*'s President, also discounts the rumours about Area 51; the movie confirms them, for military intelligence has kept this President in the dark. In homage to *JFK*, and incurring the wrath of the right-wing elite opinion journal, *The American Spectator*, *Independence Day* reveals a government conspiracy to keep secret the original alien landing.[35]

(Top) President Bill Clinton, Belfast, December 1995 (photo by Cynthia Johnson; by permission of Time/Life Syndication). (Bottom) *JFK*

The military-industrial complex gave birth to an alien form of life in the giant ant movie, Them! Produced from a mutation caused by atomic tests, the giant ants made bigger than life the invisible effects of atomic radiation, like the radioactive iodine the Department of Energy now acknowledges that its predecessor, the Atomic Energy Commission, released for two decades when, without warning or precautions, it tested atomic bombs in the Nevada desert. The radioactive iodine, present in levels greater than Chernobyl, posed a particular cancer threat to children, entering their growing bodies in their milk. Registering the anxiety that post-World War II atomic, militarised, secret government had transformed the United States – an uneasiness intensified on the far right with the end of the justificatory Cold War – Independence Day flirts with Robert Cantwell's conceit that 'the United States at the end of World War II had been invaded by its own army' that 'the war had won us.'36

From its opening shot sequence, *Independence Day* insists on the similarity between them (or *Them!*) and us. The American flag planted

*Them!*

on the moon gives way to the shadow of a giant flying saucer, as if to confirm Severen Darden's 1950s invocation of Newton's law, 'Every action has an equal and opposite reaction. Therefore, if we send space ships out to Mars, they'll send space ships back to us.'[37] The alien flying saucer has the shape of the earth communication satellites that replace it on screen. The aliens themselves are – in the words of the mad scientist who has been studying them for half a century – 'pretty much like us'. Preserved in bottles, their vulnerable, oxygen-breathing bodies could pass for human foetuses. At the other end of the biology–technology interface, the aliens' technological competence is so interchangeable with ours that our pilot can fly their aircraft and our computer whiz can penetrate their software. In addition to giving the aliens our weapons of mass destruction, the film also describes them – locusts who use up natural resources and then move on – in human, all-too-human, American national and corporate multinational terms.

The American flag on the moon, earth communications satellite dishes

*Independence Day* capitalises on a popular distrust of government so strong in the years leading up to the film that the *New York Times Magazine* mused in 1994, 'People talk as if our political system had been taken over by aliens.'[38] Obsessed with federal government conspiracies, the violent militia movement was a focus of media attention. FBI agents had shot and killed the wife and infant daughter of a far-right extremist at Ruby Ridge, Idaho in 1992. The government assaulted the Branch Davidian religious cult compound in Waco, Texas a year later. These attacks lent credence to right-wing anti-government paranoia. On the second anniversary of the incineration of the Waco Branch Davidians, 19 April 1995, as Emmerich and Devlin were about to prepare their White

House conflagration for the screen, two militia members blew up the Federal Office Building in Oklahoma City.

Audiences that cheered the White House holocaust might seem to have been mobilised by *ID4* for an assault on the political elite. The graphic destruction of American icons, generating a crowd-pleasing *frisson* more intense than any produced by the familiar science fiction fantasy air battles, did give *ID4* its peculiar appeal. But the unintended consequence of Oklahoma City was the organising principle of *Independence Day* – that the bombers acquire the alien stigma heretofore attached to the federal government. Emmerich and Devlin conceived *Independence Day* in the wake of the massive alienation from Washington that had given Republicans control of both houses of Congress in 1994

Firestorm

for the first time in forty years. By the time the film opened it was participating in what it showed: the resurrection of a youthful President from political death. Encapsulated within *ID4* is what re-elected Clinton, the mood swing from internal division and fear of decline to national self-congratulation. For like other examples of contemporary 'populism', and unlike the late nineteenth-century movement of that name, *Independence Day* serves American power in the name of attacking it. The contemporary film reverses *The Day the Earth Stood Still*, where an alien spacecraft that lands in Washington warns humans to cease endangering the universe. *The American Spectator* need not have worried, for, as with the exposure of alien and human as mirror images, the secret government conspiracy puts on screen widely-shared worries about the breakdown of difference in order to re-establish the contrast between us and them. Everyone who has seen the movie knows that the contrast takes two forms. First, they are uniform, all alike; we are multicultural. Second, they are foetal, fluid and slimy; we are men.[39]

# 4 Multiculturalism

'Given its politically correct themes and multicultural cast of characters',
the *New York Times* wants to know, how could *Independence Day* possibly
give offence?[40] Celebrated for its 'diversity', to quote Bob Dole,
*Independence Day* is actually organised around Jewish–black
reconciliation. Nostalgia for the Jewish–black alliance takes the place in
this film of equal opportunity for those post-1960s multicultural groups,
Latinos, Asians, women and gays.

Since the civil rights movement engendered women's and gay
liberation at the end of the 1960s – the same decade when the revision
of US immigration law initiated a massive population movement into the
United States – quarrels over multiculturalism have dominated American
cultural and political discourse. Responsible for more than one-third of
US population growth in the 1980s, more immigrants arrived during that
decade than in any since the early twentieth century. Instead of coming
through the front door to be welcomed by the Statue of Liberty (which
falls into New York harbour in *Independence Day*), 80% of the new
immigrants entered from the bottom and the back, i.e. Latin America
and Asia. Americanisation campaigns early in the century aimed to
assimilate what Theodore Roosevelt called the 'tangle of squabbling
nationalities' from southern and eastern Europe. The immigration
restriction bill of 1924, under the sway of racialist national origins
pseudoscience, effectively barred Slavs, Jews and Italians from entering
the United States, although the greatest stigma was still reserved for
'aliens ineligible for citizenship', 'Negroids' and 'Mongolians' (Asians).
According to the eminent historian Arthur Schlesinger, Jr., the new
immigration and demands for special validation by African-Americans,
women, lesbians and gays threaten the 'disintegration of the national
community, apartheid, Balkanization, tribalization'.[41]

The mainstream Democrats, opinion-makers and liberal academics
like Schlesinger who attack multiculturalism hardly advocate a return to
Anglo-Saxon white supremacy. They want to restore the New Deal
coalition, the World War II–civil rights alliance of European ethnics,

blacks and progressive WASPs. European immigrants and African-Americans, coming of age in the New Deal and civil rights revolutions, have generated a culturally pluralist version of the melting pot. As Schlesinger puts it, 'ethnic transfusions' have 'modified, enriched, and reconstituted' the 'Anglo-Saxon base' of the United States. 'No nation before had ever made diversity itself a source of national identity and unity,' writes Laurence Fuchs in *The American Kaleidescope*. *Independence Day* self-consciously furthers that national identity programme, and only the false counterposition between Nordic and rainbow versions of the

The statue of liberty, post-attack

United States puts the film on the multicultural side. Whereas 'the two great "world" wars of the twentieth century began as fights among European states,' in Schlesinger's view, the harmonious mix of European nationalities in the United States saved Europe in both world wars; it saves the world in *Independence Day*. That rescue operation displays the nostalgic punishing force of 'e pluribus unum' – the American motto that titles the last chapter of Schlesinger's *Disuniting of America* – for the United States comes together in *Independence Day* at the expense of the groups whose demands for recognition fragmented the New Deal/World

War II Democratic Party Unlike the xenophobic tract *Alien Nation*, *ID4* goes after extraterrestrials to make a place for immigrants. But not all ethnic, racial, and sexual identities will get equal billing.[42]

Women are most obviously restored to supporting roles in this supposedly politically correct film. The three career professionals with whom the film begins are re-subordinated to their husbands by its end. Fatally injured in the destruction of Los Angeles, the President's wife wishes in her dying words that she had surrendered to her husband's desire and returned home immediately from her business trip; here the film winks at the remaking of Hillary Clinton from independent political player to loyal spouse. The unwed black mother and stripper, having first nursed the President's injured wife, then marries her black pilot as his send-off into space; here the film solves the problem of single motherhood now blamed for family disintegration and black poverty. The ambitious Presidential press secretary (here the film has a go at women who sacrifice family to career) has divorced her Jewish computer-whiz husband before the film begins. Handholding and a subjective camera shot (from the press secretary's point of view) during the black couple's wedding ceremony show the divorced David still wearing his wedding ring. In what in effect becomes a double ceremony, David's ex-wife repledges herself to her man. Supportive paternal figures (David's actual father and the President's General) deepen the patriarchal line and sustain the three heroes, who redeem themselves in action; there are no older women to threaten the young men or support their wives.

Jasmine (Vivica Fox) nurses the President's wife (Mary McDonnell)

These traditional family values, winning the Dole/Clinton/William Bennett seal of approval, are entirely on the surface. But they also resolve a deeper boundary anxiety over sexual difference, about which the film is entirely self-conscious but which no reviewer has addressed. The career women who open the film split into domesticated and dying females on the one hand, a monstrous extraterrestrial 'mothership' and its foetal weapons on the other. A homophobic homoerotics will climax *Independence Day*, as American pilots enter two orifices, one of the alien mothership and the other of a 'second generation' attacker, and exit from only one. To achieve that rebirth, *ID4* travels through the arena of difference other than the sexual, the multicultural, where the film is also ahead of its reviewers. Just as the movie's gender politics is a cover for its sexual politics, so a retrograde, World War II multi-ethnicity has diverted attention from the motion picture's restrictive contemporary multiculturalism.

Although more than one 1940s movie violated the rule, no black man could serve in the multi-ethnic World War II Jim Crow platoon. But thanks to the identification of Nazi anti-Semitism with American Jim Crow, the Jewish–black civil rights alliance reached its highpoint during and after the war. Since that alliance shattered so publicly in the late 1960s over black power and anti-Zionist 'third worldism', an enormous amount of ink has been spilled over what went wrong and who was to blame. With the displacement of politics by culture in the post-Watergate era, Hollywood itself has featured as a site of black–Jewish conflict. Black anti-

Wedding participants David (Jeff Goldblum) and Constance (Margaret Colin)

*Bataan*'s World War II platoon; Kenneth Spencer as Wesley Epps

Semites periodically discover Jewish control of the motion picture business. The year before Emmerich and Devlin conceived *ID4*, an Oakland black high school class was expelled from a matinee of *Schindler's List* when some of the teenagers seemed to be cheering the Nazis on. Exaggerated attention to such incidents blots out not only continuing co-operative organisational relations and shared political attitudes among blacks and Jews, but also the wider range of contemporary American multiculturalism. It is as if restoring the black–Jewish alliance would overcome the widely-advertised disuniting of America.[43]

Although Jewish–black tension never appears directly in the film, its traces are everywhere. Interracial individual friendship, like that established between the Jeff Goldblum and Will Smith characters (David Levinson and Captain Steven Hiller), is by now the ubiquitous Hollywood answer to group racial inequality. In recent films, however, Jeff Goldblum has twice betrayed his black buddies – Lawrence Fishburne in *Deep Cover* and Samuel Jackson in *The Great White Hype* – at what turns out to be his own expense. The condition for individual Jewish–black bonding, moreover, is not only the threat of world destruction, but also the actual obliteration of the urban habitats – New York, Los Angeles, Washington, DC – in which these population groups live *en masse*. The film brings that message home by singling out individual Jews and blacks for annihilation – a single Jew as neurasthenic

Captain Hiller (Will Smith) and David flying the alien spacecraft

Bringing the Torah

Julius (Judd Hirsch), Constance and David

hysteric, several blacks as anonymous observers of the alien spacecrafts. Perhaps Ken Khachigian, Dole's senior California adviser, was making a coded ethnic joke when he responded to a query about the millions who die in *Independence Day* with the quip, 'but they're all liberals'.[44]

Those who believe that the end of legalised Jim Crow equalised the playing field between whites and blacks insist that the law be 'colour blind'. Themselves blind to the law's differential impact on differently situated racialised groups, post-civil rights advocates of legal colour-blindedness are hardly colour blind themselves. They point to individual minority success as evidence for equality of opportunity. From the Supreme Court (Clarence Thomas) to Hollywood, visible minority individuals thus stand in for the absence of substantive racial equality. Hollywood heroes, like those in US school textbooks, remained white for years in defiance of American diversity. The New Hollywood, coming especially to feature black male action heroes in buddy roles, is in part responding belatedly to the civil rights revolution. But far from progressing in a new multicultural direction, it is putting on screen the ancient dream of adventure in classic American literature, the escape from women and everyday social routine into interracial male camaraderie.[45]

Starting out in entirely separate worlds, the Will Smith and Jeff Goldblum characters are brought together by catastrophe. A tight two-shot establishes that they will fly together and alone into alien territory, and extended by-play in close alien–spacecraft quarters ('We got to work on our communication') consummates their integration. Smith and Goldblum play what James Wolcott calls 'the Cornel West and Michael Lerner of extraterrestial *tikkun*'; Wolcott is alluding to the public 'conversations' staged between the *Tikkun* editor and the black activist intellectual to rectify Jewish–black misunderstandings. When Jewish sons Americanised through playing black, as in the first talking picture, the blackface *The Jazz Singer*, religious Jewish fathers stood in the way. In the widely-publicised contemporary conflicts between Brooklyn black and Hasidic Jewish communities, by contrast, Jewish sons choose their fathers' side. David's father, however, is a religious go-between. In a gift exchange that rubs our noses in the racial politics of *Tikkun*'s Jewish renewal, a black lab assistant – white-coated inheritor of the black servants of an earlier era – rushes up with yarmulke and torah for the religious ceremony that will consecrate the Jewish–black journey into space. David's father reciprocates with his own burnt offering: two cigars for Captain Hiller's anticipated victory ritual with David. David's father, Julius, is not the only Jewish male hysteric in this film. He is joined by David's panicked sidekick, Marty, who calls his mother from under his desk and his psychoanalyst ('Dr Katz') from his car phone. These stereotypical Jewish neurasthenics serve to masculinise, by contrast, the borderline nerdy Jewish hero.[46]

Julius and Marty have taken criticism as stereotypes, but at least they come from a recognisably Jewish milieu. David and Captain Hiller, by contrast, exemplify the new ethnicity of free choice 'concerned with the symbols of ethnic cultures rather than with the cultures themselves'. Whereas the black pilot weds endogamously, David goes one better than his *Jazz Singer* predecessor by twice marrying his (so far as we can tell) non-Jewish wife. 'No longer, then, need there be any contradiction between being American and asserting an ethnic identity,' as one sociologist puts it, because symbolic ethnicity has emancipated itself from deeply-rooted communal attachments.[47]

Classic Hollywood producers furthered their assimilation project by preventing Jews from playing Jews on screen; Jewish actors in ethnically marked roles mostly appeared as Italians and Indians. Illustrating the moguls' dream of Americanisation, *The Jazz Singer* was the exception that proved the rule. Jewish players in the New Hollywood now often take centre stage, as exemplified by Jeff Goldblum's starring roles in three all-time top grossers, *Independence Day*, *Jurassic Park* and *The Lost World* (the *Jurassic Park* sequel he filmed after finishing *ID4*). But as Jews become stand-ins for European ethnics, they trade in their historic substance for the symbols of American nationalism.[48]

Still, Jewish computer whiz and black trash-talking fighter restore the Jewish–black alliance by sticking to their familiar, second-level-of-power, roles. Jew is mouth as nervous brain, black is mouth as boastful body. To David's anxious question, 'Do you really think you can fly that thing?' Hiller ripostes, 'You really think you can do all that bullshit you just said?' Whereas black power wins in Jeff Goldblum's previous black buddy films, the WASP President takes charge in *Independence Day*. *ID4*'s ethnic politics resurrect the New Deal–Great Society coalition of Jew, black and public-spirited WASP. (New Yorkers might imagine what it would take to bring back together John Lindsay, New York's elite protestant liberal mayor of the 1960s, Ed Koch, the Jewish reformer turned neoconservative who replaced him, and Charles Rangel, the long-term Congressman from Harlem who continues to occupy the shrunken left wing of the Democratic Party.)

Government secrets: Secretary of Defense Nimziki (James Rebhorn) and Dr Okun (Brent Spiner)

The President takes charge by firing his Defense Secretary, the nuclear-trigger happy, former CIA chief named Nimziki, who informed him neither of the Search for Extraterrestrial Institute nor of the original alien desert landing. Although named for Joe Nimziki, MGM's head of advertising, in body type and name Nimziki is reminiscent of Zbigniew Brzezinski, the Polish emigré cold warrior, professor (my former teacher) and Carter national security adviser. Brzezinski is the author of a futuristic, technophiliac science fiction fantasy masquerading as political science, *Between Two Ages: America's Role in the Technetronic Era*. His *ID4* role pays homage to Brzezinski's real-life counterpart and rival, Dr Henry Kissinger, himself the model for Dr Strangelove.[49]

A Polish-American villain may seem to violate the advertised multiculturalism of *Independence Day*. But whereas the anti-anti-Communist referent signals that we are expansively beyond the Cold War, the ethnic signifier points to the narrow spectrum of the movie's rainbow coalition. Jewish shtick and black rap are so prominent in *Independence Day* because they stand in for contemporary American diversity. The black–Jewish relation is an old American story, our familiar triumph and tragedy. At once occluded by and posed against it are the recently intensified multicultural invasions, those of the Asian and Latino aliens for whom – as the film briefly and deliberately lets us know – its own aliens stand.

The first human to hear the alien signal is an Asian-American working at the Search for Extraterrestrial Institute; he calls over members of the groups that will displace him, one Jewish man, one black man and one white woman. Then he and his people (with the exception of a single victim of the Angeleno holocaust) exit the film. Just as with the elimination of charred Hiroshimans from the Enola Gay exhibit, so Asian disappearance is required to restore American victory culture. Although the destruction of American cities may imply reparation for the US bombs dropped on Asia from Japan to Iraq, visible Asians would open old wounds. They would serve not only as an unwelcome historical mnemonic device, but also as a contemporary anxiety-raiser. Looking backward, 'The Rising Sun' evokes World War II and Hiroshima (for example, in the words of the 1946 Homer Harris/Muddy Waters 'Atomic Bomb Blues'). Facing forward (as in the Michael Crichton book and Philip Kaufman movie), *Rising Sun* points to the economically and technologically advanced ascendant Asian empire that only yesterday was seen as overtaking an America in decline.[50]

Ancestor of *ID4*'s Asian, a lone Mexican is among the first three men vaporised by *War of the Worlds*' Martians, leaving the rest of the film lily-white. Latinos, by contrast, have a role to play in *Independence Day*; they link the illegal aliens of American politics (often imagined outside

Father and son: Russell Casse (Randy Quaid) and Miguel (James Duval)

the movie not as labouring in our fields but as unproductive locusts depleting our resources) to the space aliens of American film. With one stunning exception that proves this associative rule, Latinos and Spanish place-names merely supply an occasional spot of local colour. But Russell Casse (Randy Quaid), the former Vietnam pilot who claims to have been abducted by aliens, has fathered two Chicano children. As Donald Pease has pointed out, they displace the more likely Asian progeny of a Vietnam vet, shifting the unresolved Vietnam syndrome onto contemporary political terrain.[51]

*Independence Day* did not originate the conflation of extraterritorial aliens and nuclear danger. A random sample of one episode of the popular television hospital show, *Chicago Hope*, features a burned, disfigured Mexican who seems to claim she has been impregnated by aliens. The pregnancy and alien parent are real, but they are combined in one body, for the Mexican herself turns out to be an illegal alien. As for the burns, she received them by scavenging at a dump site for radioactive waste. Perhaps the television hospital show's prefiguration of *ID4* illustrates shared cultural associations, although Margaret Colin – first a terminally ill doctor on *Chicago Hope* and then *ID4*'s presidential press secretary – may supply the missing link.[52]

*Chicago Hope*'s alien baby is delivered safely at the happy ending of the show. In localising nuclear danger on the body that is then delivered from it, *Chicago Hope* anticipates the climactic deliverance of *Independence Day*. *Chicago Hope* confined invasion to a female body. Opening up a male warrior instead, *ID4* makes him the instrument of world redemption. For the aliens from outer space who did not impregnate the illegal alien have entered Russell Casse. Russell has broken down, rumour has it, not from Vietnam post-traumatic stress disorder but from alien sexual abuse. *Independence Day* replaces the troubling earthly histories of Vietnam veterans – as POW victims and illegitimate fathers – with the fantasy of extraterrestrial abduction. The disorienting address, 'Your father', that first connects the Chicano teenager to the redneck cropduster is clarified, in the film's psycho-logic, by alien carnal aggression. The alien–Casse liaison, moreover, fills the space of the missing Chicana mother. (As if further to link the *Chicago Hope* episode to *Independence Day*, an 'operating room nurse' who attended *ID4*'s opening night explained that she 'loved the scientific part, and I do think this sort of thing could happen. I think we probably have captured aliens. I believe that the Government knows more than they can let people know.')[53]

Freud's Schreber, the locus classicus of paranoia, hallucinated sexual mistreatment originating in outer space; Russell Casse turns out to testify not to the sexual delusions of paranoia but to the truth of alien power. Severen Darden, remember, had warned that aliens would react to our action of sending ships into space by sending their space ships back to us. *Independence Day* comments on the question that was Darden's corollary of Newton's second law, 'Do we want those monsters marrying our children?' For Russell's Chicano children are products of one alien miscegenation, and his breakdown is the product of the other. As California governor Pete Wilson was winning re-election on a platform of denying citizenship to the children of illegal aliens born on American soil – adopted at the 1996 Republican national convention – *Chicago Hope*'s pregnant Mexican fulfilled her political destiny by giving birth in the United States. Russell turns the tables on his alien invaders by delivering the battle-turning nuclear strike.[54]

## 5 The Virus

The invasion of the body politic that has pulverised human bodies
reaches half its twin climax through Russell, the other half through the
team of African-American and Jew. To prepare that climax, which we will
be examining in detail, *ID4* focuses on the vulnerable individual body.
Obliteration of American national icons in this family values film,
however, contrasts with sanitised images of disintegrated human beings.
The most graphic bodily operation, also paying homage to television
hospital shows, dissects a captured alien instead. But what looks like
cutting open a skull and body to expose organs and viscera turns out
simply to remove the alien's 'biomechanical suit'. For the alien wears a
'carapace', 'vulnerable flesh covered by a protective shell'.[55] Undressed
but still intact, it remains tentacled and dangerous. Whereas sensate
bodily borders make the human interior vulnerable to external
penetration, body armour insulates the alien.

By the same token, an 'invisible shield' that renders impotent our
nuclear missiles protects the alien body politic. *ID4* borrows its aliens'
invisible shield from three sources. The first, to whose significance we will
return, is the Cold War Colgate toothpaste advertisement in which a
Gardol 'invisible shield' repelled halitosis-producing bacteria. The second
is the 'protective blister' in *War of the Worlds*. *Independence Day* repeats
two battle scenes from the earlier movie, one in which the alien force field

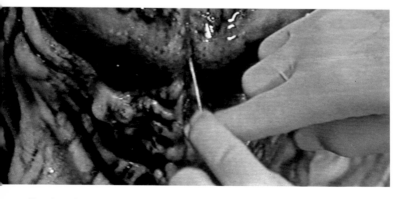

Alien dissection

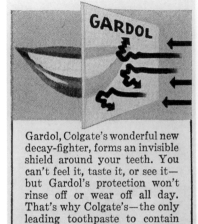

Gardol, Colgate's wonderful new decay-fighter, forms an invisible shield around your teeth. You can't feel it, taste it, or see it— but Gardol's protection won't rinse off or wear off all day. That's why Colgate's—the only leading toothpaste to contain Gardol—gives the surest protection ever offered by any toothpaste!

Colgate toothpaste's invisible shield (by permission of Colgate/Palmolive)

*War of the Worlds*

repels our combat weapons, the other in which an atomic bomb fails to harm the aliens' presence on the ground. Close in time to Hiroshima, *War of the Worlds* depicted the lone pilot of a lone, Enola Gay-like plane which, failing to destroy the aliens, still left behind a mushroom cloud; *ID4* instead invokes, as the third source of its invisible shield, Star Wars. Reagan's Strategic Defense Initiative comprised, along with the masculine hard bodies featured in Reaganite entertainment, the defence policy and popular culture responses to Vietnam defeat. Film graphics illustrating the alien's invisible shield actually imitate the advertisement for Star Wars (the missile defence system not the movie), promoted by a group calling itself 'High Frontier'. Desensitising borders is an autistic means of defence which anaesthetises the interior in the name of protecting it. *Independence Day* awards that fantasised invulnerability to the enemy.[56]

Stripped of its biomechanical suit, the tentacled alien violates human borders. Instead of crossing linguistic barriers with hand gestures and body language, as in David's Jewish joke, the alien invades the President's mind and body through ESP. Eyes – the President's stand-in for the film spectators' – prove vulnerable points of entry through which the alien reads human thoughts and imposes its own. Visual assault informs the President that the aliens, devouring locusts, will make us their prey.

*ID4*'s cyborg manifesto makes permeable the borders between the biological and the mechanical, the human and the non-human, the individual corporeal and the corporate, in the service of apparent alien invulnerability. Devlin and Emmerich cast Brent Spiner as their alien-investigating scientist, capitalising on his role as the 'endearing and ever-so-handy android', Data, in *Star Trek*. Spiner is by design 'nearly unrecognisable' as the maniacal Dr Okun, however, for *ID4*'s extraterrestrials render malevolent Data's happy synthesis of technological competence and biological feeling. Although humans may think they have mastered technology, it renders them helpless in alien hands, the tentacles that strangle Dr Okun.[57]

But one alien invasive weapon turns out to provide its own point of entry into the heart, or rather the bowels, of the alien body politic. In *2001: A Space Odyssey*, the computer Hal is 'the brain and essential nervous system of the ship'. When, perhaps under alien influence, Hal turns against the crew, the sole surviver of the space ship has 'to cut his higher brain functions'.[58] *Independence Day* combines that computer life and death with the *War of the Worlds*' bacterial revenge. The 'machines' of war having failed in *War of the Worlds*, scientists turn to 'some biological approach' instead. They abandon massive retaliation in an effort to utilise germs, the tiny, invisible weapons that reside within the body. David's forebear, coded Jewish refugee by her central European accent, discovers under a microscope that the aliens' vulnerability lies in their 'blood crystals'.

The human germs that fell 1950s aliens in *War of the Worlds* enter *Independence Day* by way of Jewish hypochondria, for when David's father nags him about getting a cold, David gets the idea of giving the aliens one. Experimentally demonstrating how to disable an invisible shield, David explains, 'I gave it a cold. I gave it a virus.' As in *War of the Worlds*, the 'littlest things … upon this earth' will destroy the invaders. But scientists turn out to be helpless in *War of the Worlds* and only 'a miracle of … divine intervention' saves humanity. *Independence Day* prayer, by contrast, empowers its human heroes. Beginning with David, they seize control of the miniaturised, cyborg field of postmodern combat.

Telling a black computer tech, 'We have work to do,' David explains, 'If we plant a virus into that mothership, it's going to filter down into all the ships below.' David had discovered that the aliens were 'using our satellites against us' as 'a signal hidden inside our own satellite system' beamed their countdown signal around the earth. Now he proposes to use the aliens' computer-operated defence system against them. His computer virus will disable the invisible shields that protect the mothership and all its progeny. 'Just how exactly do we infect the mothership with this virus?' asks Nimziki incredulously. The answer is that David and Captain Hiller will fly a captured alien spacecraft back into the mothership's body, dock inside her and upload the virus into what *2001* had called her 'brain and essential nervous system'. Thinking that Hiller and David are alien pilots coming home, the mothership opens up her giant V-shaped orifice to invite their tiny projectile inside – through a long tunnel and into an interior space designed with an

The sperm parachute jump, *Everything You Always Wanted to Know About Sex …*

*E.T.*

'organic', 'underwatery feel', 'with plenty of blobby and rounded edges' (as Will Smith describes it) and populated by hundreds of other tiny ships. The episode picks up where Woody Allen's *Everything You Always Wanted to Know about Sex* left off a quarter-century earlier, with the parachute jump of sperm into a welcoming female body; now the single out-of-place black sperm among the multitude of white has progressed to equal billing. Recalling *Sex* at the mothership's entrance, the scene deliberately pays homage to the 1978 science fiction horror film, *Alien*. *Alien*'s space ship computer is called 'Mother', its human crew enters the alien ship through a vaginal opening, and one crew member drops down into a giant womb-like, heated egg chamber.[59]

Although Captain Hiller engages one alien in hand-to-tentacle combat, the reviewer who 'wouldn't bet on [the] gender' of the aliens has spotted their polymorphous perversity. It begins in the womb. So strong is the Hollywood convention that aliens resemble foetuses that a recent review of one *Independence Day* spin-off is titled 'Fetal Attraction'. *Close Encounters of the Third Kind* and *E.T.* are in love with their foetal extraterrestrials; they push the New Hollywood's sentimentalisation of childhood innocence back as far as it can go. The foetal, however, also invokes the body's anxiety-making fluid borders, ambiguous sexuality and vulnerability to maternal power. As the review title suggests, foetal attraction is the double of *Fatal Attraction*, the backlash film of female sexual revenge, for *ID4*'s foetal aliens serve the dystopic extraterrestrial maternal body.[60]

The foetal aliens

Science fiction horror, Barbara Creed writes, locates the alien threat in the 'monstrous feminine', the archaic maternal power over reproduction, life and death. Intuiting that connection on the morning that he loaded the Hiroshima atom bomb, Colonel Paul W. Tibbets, Jr. painted the name of his mother, Enola Gay, underneath his pilot's window. Alamagordo scientists had christened his bomb Little Boy. When the aircraft had 'laid its egg, the Atomic Age was born', as the Smithsonian National Air Museum's curator put it in 1949. Fresh from the birthing ceremony that had launched the atomic age, the Enola Gay was being welcomed into America's 'Valhalla of the Air'. So soon after the completion of the Wagner–Hitler ring cycle, however, the National Air Museum's Valhalla betrayed anxiety beneath its triumphalism, for Valhalla identified the birth of the atomic age with the death of the Gods, Götterdämmerung. So the Enola Gay was hidden away, parked at Wendover Airport in the Utah desert. It was there – and at Hughes Aircraft in Culver City 'where top-secret weapons were designed and built during the Cold War' – that Emmerich and Devlin filmed their Roswell scenes. The massive projection of *Independence Day* turns the destructive power of the mothership against its alien source.[61]

'We're in,' says David, now meaning not into the body of the mothership but into its computer. 'Uploading virus,' says the computer screen. The computer, cybernetic virus takes its name from the animal, biological virus. 'How does a virus work?' asks a popular magazine article. 'Once inside a host cell, … the virus insinuates itself into the cell's replicative processes by attaching to its DNA or RNA, and tricks the cell into producing more viruses through the same mechanisms the cell uses to copy its own genes.'[62] Replicating the code of the organism – DNA, WP5 or ID4 – against itself, viruses disable the organism's immune system, leaving it vulnerable to opportunistic invasion.

'When they invade our bodies, viruses get into the very structure of our cells and wait, dormant but deadly, to emerge when our defenses are down.' Circulating among biological virus, computer virus and war, *ID4* is drawing on a long history of cultural associations. 'Every minute of every day wars rage within our bodies', begins the *National*

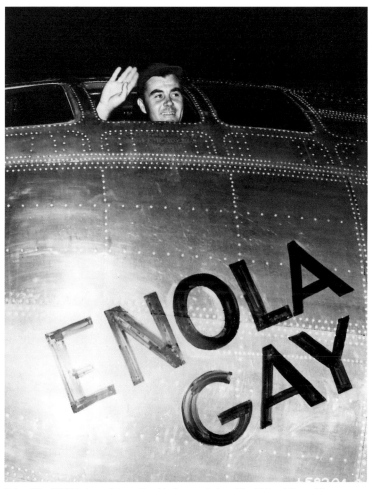

Colonel Paul W. Tibbets and his mothership (by permission of the National Air and Space Museum)

*Geographic* feature, 'Our Immune System: The Wars Within'. Body and body politic anxieties already fed off one another in the Cold War 1950s, as the 'endless war metaphors' of both lay and scientific literature depicted immunology with the language and visual imagery of military invasion. In Cindy Patton's summary, which takes us from Cold War germs and cancers to AIDS,

Suppressor cells were there to stop killer cells when the 'enemy' had been vanquished, overriding revolt (cancer) by renegade 'self' cells. Immunology was

Inside the mothership

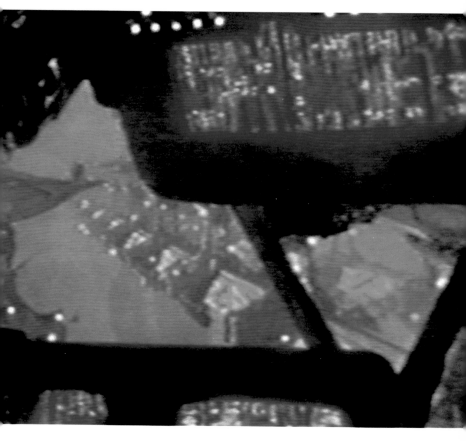

not so much about the Other as about the marginally different that had already been admitted to close proximity. ... People would now visualize their bodies as filled with tiny defending armies whose mission was to return the 'self' to the precarious balance of health. ... If you failed to defend yourself against germs, it was because you did not succeed in managing your army. The metaphoric slippage between self-management and military management echoed anxieties about 'losing' in Vietnam ... (there were of course many Vietnam veterans among early diagnosed cases of AIDS); thus both AIDS and the war are cast as masculine experiences in highly eroticized male-only zones.[63]

Donna Haraway has suggested that modern immunology moved into high science when it reworked the combat metaphors of World War II (battles, territory, enemy) into the language of post-modern warfare (command, communication, control, transmission, messages). Borrowed from nuclear strategy and counter-insurgency warfare, these terms brought disease contagion into the atomic age. Cold warriors attacked the 'Communist virus'. Nuclear war anxieties entered the body invisibly during the Cold War, directly through radiation damage and displaced – see *Dr. Strangelove* – into such paranoias as that over fluoridation. But underneath these fears of body penetration lay the big bang.[64]

*Independence Day* updates such language in the service of total war. 'We're fighting for our right to live,' proclaims the President, elevating his 4 July over the mere pursuit of liberty in the original. Sanctioning the shift from high ideals to biological survival, this reduction to the life process culminates the sustained national emergency from the end of World War II that justified a military industrial expansion devoid of any higher purpose.[65] *Independence Day* gratifies the wish for apocalyptic triumph aborted when the Cold War 'empire of evil' ended not with a bang but with a whimper. But post-Cold War anxieties experienced as personal rather than political fuel the retrospective force of the victory wish; from toxic wastes and environmental cancers to epidemic diseases, no evil empire is now their source and no apocalpytic world-ending big bang their culmination. The single giant enemy of *Independence Day*, who can be met in battle and defeated – Ahab's whale – is actually an imaginary defence against the proliferation of multiple, disorganising, diffuse points of bodily vulnerability.

According to the *Time* cover story on *Independence Day*, whereas 1950s science fictions like *Invasion of the Body Snatchers* allegorised foreign threats to the United States, now the 'alien is inside, a virus of one kind or another'. 'One kind or another' is *Time*'s evasion of AIDS, the 'science fiction' illness (as *National Geographic* called it), the one contemporary viral disease to which the terms apocalypse and holocaust are, with the end of the Cold War and the recession of the nuclear balance of terror, now applied. As pictured in the *National Geographic*, for example, 'Before the defending T cell can mobilize the troops, the virus disables it. ... One by one, its clones begin to infect nearby T cells. Slowly but inexorably the body loses the very sentinels that should be alerting the rest of the immune system. ... The enemy can run free.' Its presence in *National Geographic* attests to the fact that HIV is the alien virus, originating elsewhere – in Haiti, in Africa, among monkeys, in humanly unnatural acts within the 'vulnerable rectum' rather than the 'rugged vagina'. *Independence Day* takes the alien virus and turns it against the alien. Given the culturally constrained contemporary free association between viruses and death, when David plants his computer virus, he is entering the field of AIDS.[66]

Clinton's 'wimp' reputation originated from his vexed relationship to gays in the armed forces, a memory revived by the homoerotic byplay in *ID4*'s military venue. 'You need to, like, kiss some serious booty to get ahead,' Hiller's buddy Jimmy (Harry Connick, Jr.) tells him in the locker room. Urging Hiller to break off with the stripper if he wants to be accepted into NASA, Jimmy kneels down and mimes kissing his buddy's ass. Discovering the engagement ring Hiller plans to give his girlfriend, Jimmy, still on his knees – seizes it and pantomimes his own gay marriage proposal. Surprising them in the act and pretending to have stumbled on a love scene, a third pilot mimes a version of Clinton's 'Don't ask, don't tell.' 'You scared man?' asks Hiller soon after, as the pilots are briefed for their first alien attack. 'Nope,' replies Jimmy, and then, crying 'Hold me,' drops his head on his black buddy's shoulder.

Jimmy is to Hiller as Marty is to David. Casting Harvey Feirstein as David's sidekick was part of the advertised multiculturalism of *ID4*; Feirstein plays what one critic calls '(surprise!) the gay office pansy'. Whereas Feirstein, who had won Tony awards for *Torch Song Trilogy* and *Cage Aux Folles*, was known as a 'gay rights activist', Connick's interest in New Orleans jazz advertised him as a crossover racial performer. *ID4* was using Connick to play sexual crossover as well. As the gay black con artist in *Six Degrees of Separation*, Will Smith had famously refused to kiss a man on screen. Not wanting to be confused with his role, Smith had disobeyed his director, Fred Schepisi, and followed Denzel Washington's advice instead. The earlier role left behind its safe residue, none the less. Casting Smith with Connick, *Independence Day* was paying homage to the interracial male homoeroticism of blackface minstrelsy and classic American literature.[67]

In their first producer/director collaboration, *Stargate* – the science fiction amalgam of *Star Wars, Indiana Jones* and *The Ten Commandments* whose surprise success enabled Emmerich and Devlin to make *Independence Day* – the bi-racial Jaye Davidson and his dark-skinned minions presided over the evil Egyptian kingdom. The film-makers were capitalising on Davidson's tranvestite notoriety as the woman who turns out to have a penis in *The Crying Game*. Primping before the camera, a beautiful, sinister boy/girl, Davidson is the dark double of *Stargate*'s distinctly unmacho protagonist, the young scientist who will mature into *ID4*'s David. Shifting from Jaye Davidson as villain to Will Smith as hero, *ID4* rescues race from homosex; it also treats its gay sidekicks affectionately. But as in its mass destruction of populations and patriotic icons, and in its operating-room prurient interest, *Independence Day* plays with forbidden desire in the service of normalisation. Making same-sex flirtation a stage in the growth toward heterosexual manhood, and itself on the road to a larger perverse sexual climax, the film kills Marty and Jimmy off.[68]

Like the third *Independence Day* queer, the flaming Angeleno queen who welcomes the aliens, Marty is incinerated; his last words are 'Oh, crap!' Jimmy and Hiller, failing to 'whip E.T.'s ass', never get to smoke their victory cigars together. 'Don't get premature on me,' says Hiller when Jimmy pretends to light up his cigar before their mission is completed, but Jimmy sacrifices himself to save his buddy. David replaces him. Although the double marriage ceremony has already inoculated the black–Jewish buddies against queering, the decisive split of normative heterosexuality from perversion only comes at the double climax of the film.

After David and Captain Hiller plant their virus inside the mothership, the other pilots fire nuclear missiles through the disabled invisible shields. A failed post-Gulf War Chief Executive, on the George

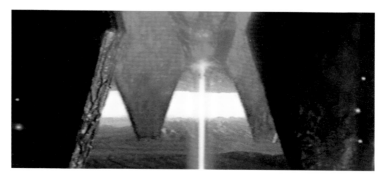

Bush model, the President redeems himself as a combat pilot in *ID4*'s virtual war. But although the mothership is damaged and many baby ships are blown up, the American planes run out of missiles before the alien's 'primary weapon' is destroyed. From inside a 'second generation' attack ship now opens up the giant orifice that will reign down destruction.[69] At this moment the *Alien*/Enola Gay monstrous feminine merges with the phallic Götterdämmerung that climaxes *Dr. Strangelove, Or How I learned to Stop Worrying and Love the Bomb*. Convinced that Communist aliens have contaminated his bodily fluids, General Jack D.

(Top) The primary weapon
(Bottom) J.J. 'King' Kong (Slim Pickens) in *Dr. Strangelove*

Ripper locks his squadron into nuclear attack. Colonel Mandrake (Peter Sellers) solves the code – POE for Purity of Essence – that will countermand General Ripper's instructions. One plane's command and control system has been hit by enemy fire, however, and does not receive the orders to abort. Undeterred when the plane's bomb-release mechanism malfunctions, the character played by Slim Pickens releases its weapon himself. Waving his cowboy hat in the air and with the bomb between his legs, he rides the bomb down to its target setting off a Russian doomsday machine and bringing the world to an end.

*Independence Day* repeats that scene, with Dennis Quaid in the Slim Pickens role. 'They did all kinds of experiments on me,' Russell has

told a TV interviewer. 'When they took him up in the space ship, the aliens abused him sexually,' it is rumoured, as if to confirm Jack D. Ripper's paranoia. Russell is not the only victim of alien sexual abuse, for sexual violation figures prominently in reports of extraterrestrial abduction. Although most abductees are women, men also emphasise the 'rape-like character of the trauma', the 'penetration by thin, metallic, penis-like instruments'. Parental violation and helplessness in the face of technological power come together on the bodies of prototypical abductees. Alien sexual abuse feminises men. Now, says Russell, 'it's payback time.' Only he among the American squadron has a missile remaining; he aims it at the alien's primary weapon, visually imaged as a bodily orifice with leg-like protrusions on either side. When Russell's

'Hello boys, I'm back!'

release mechanism jams, on the *Dr. Strangelove* model, he also refuses to abort his mission. 'Tell my children I love them,' says the American kamikaze, redeeming one set of aliens by destroying another. As the camera cuts between the pilot and his Chicano son, Russell shouts, 'All right you alien assholes. In the words of my generation, up yours.' Speaking his last words, 'Hello Boys, I'm back!' Russell Casse pays back the alien sex abusers by flying up the alien asshole.[70]

Assholes are no longer a forbidden object of attention in Hollywood. They dominate, for example, two stories in the 1994 critical and cult hit, *Pulp Fiction*: in one, a former Vietnam POW reports hiding his father's watch in his anal cavity to protect it from the VietCong; in the other, he saves a black crime boss from attempted anal rape. These episodes point to the central denoument, John Travolta shot taking a crap. Family entertainment, *Independence Day* contains nothing so visually graphic, but the meaning of its climax could not be more explicit. The distinguishing feature of the science fiction film of alien possession, suggests Carol Clover, is that the body in question – 'penetrated, invaded, and colonized … convulsed by some alien force' – is male.[71] With its coy conjunction of alien sexual abuse, *Alien* and *Strangelove*, *ID4* appropriates the alien possession film genre without exhibiting its horror. And just as David's multiplying virus turns the reproductive tables against the mothership, so Russell's doomsday climax penetrates the 'vulnerable rectum', opens it up, and explodes inside the mothership's progeny.

Because humans are born '*inter urinas et faeces*', in Freud's invocation of Augustine, their conflation of the three female orifices produces fantasies of anal birth. The discovery that the maternal phallus is missing, Freud argued, allies anal birth, homosexual desire and castration, since the male child imagines that castration is the consequence of sexual desire for the father. In 1950s Cold War homophobia – when more alleged gays than Communists were fired as security risks, and one psychiatrist complained that just because homosexuality was as prevalent as the common cold didn't make either one normal – the dominating mother was the demonic parent who queered her sons. It may be, as Lee Edelman argues, that Freud's alliance of homosexuality with castration defended normative heterosexuality against the discovery that anal sex produces a second erect penis not a castrated one. By the same token, assigning castrating penis envy to the mother of the queer served homophobic misogyny. As these doctrinal prohibitions against anal sex recede, AIDS hystericises the anus as a phobic sexual object. What Schreber did for Freud, AIDS for us names the male hysteria over bodily penetration.[72]

Kane, the *Alien* crew member who cracks open the alien egg, is himself impregnated by an alien tentacle. After incubating inside him, the alien bursts out of his bloody chest in a horrifying monstrous birth. *ID4* inverts that extended birth trauma primal scene by twice splitting it in two. In the reincarnation of *Alien*'s impregnation, the Area 51 scientist who dissects the alien's biomechanical suit is strangled by an alien tentacle, and the President is penetrated through his eyes. In the reincarnation of *Alien*'s birth, a reversal, Russell re-enters and blows up one orifice. He thereby preserves – the split within the split – the masculinity of the buddies who emerge from the other. Dave unplugs

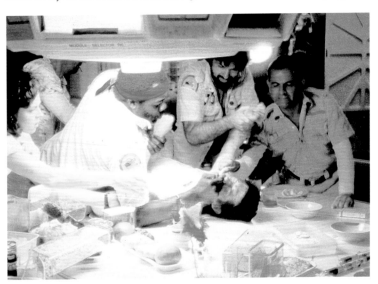

The alien delivery, *Alien* (The Ronald Grant Archive)

Hal in *2001*, grows old on Jupiter and dies alone. Kane dies in giving monstrous birth, and the *Alien* computer, 'Mother', turns out, like Hal, to be working against the crew. But the *ID4* computer that, imitating Hal, also says, 'Good morning, Dave' remains the servant of its human operater. After David and Hiller disable the invisible shields, they fire a nuclear missile into the mothership's 'cortex' to force her to let them go. As the digitally produced, visually imaged, barred V – the giant vagina dentata – is rapidly contracting, they fly out through the tiny hole just in time. Smoking their cigars together, they escape entombment in the mothership. 'I love you,' David tells Hiller, and the men return to their wives. God had turned him into a woman, Schreber imagined, so that he could give birth to a new race of men. Bifurcating the two maternal orifices at its climax, *Independence Day* allies anal penetration with death, escapes maternal power and rescues heterosexuality. The return of the

(Top) The mothership's entrance/exit
(Bottom) The mothership's shadow

Jewish–black alliance also saves Clinton's Democratic Party, menaced by the defection of southern whites, for the anal explosion wipes out not only the aliens but also the Reagan Democrat, the good old boy (Randy Quaid had played Lyndon Johnson in a television miniseries) who had illegal congress with them.[73]

The world anus, the mouth of hell, excretes into the inferno the tortured bodies of the damned in the Last Judgment panels of William Bennett's medieval sacred order. When Hollywood fulfils Bennett's injunction, then neither our Enola Gay nor the alien primary weapon gives birth to mass destruction. In Ron Kovic's autobiography, *Born on the Fourth of July*, filmed by Oliver Stone, the paraplegic Vietnam Vet lost his 'dead dick' in Vietnam. America is 'reborn on the fourth of July', as the *New Yorker* headed its review of *Independence Day*, when the miscegenating Russell's sacrifice up one orifice delivers Jew and African-American out the other.[74]

## 6 The Virtual War of the Worlds

Microscopic, invisible, computer chips, viruses and germs; visual imaging systems for viral detection; the multiplication of moving images, biological viruses and digitalised computer information – all these translate disease, computers and film into one another. 'Our minds are colonized by images. Images are a virus,' write two commentators taking off from a *Vogue* article on viruses. 'In the absence of a truly unique, first-person experience in one's own RNA-coded memory cells, how can one feel confident about one's basic identity?' they ask, making the fashion magazine itself into the enemy. Pointing out that Rupert Murdoch advertised his own Fox and Star TV network in the film that he financed, Time worries that 'movie makers ... control us, as cunningly as an *ID4* alien running a mindscan on a puny Earthling,' as if *Time* itself were not the tool of a competing intergalactal force, Time-Warner, the very object of Dole's original attack on Hollywood. Media centralisation into a few giant corporations that combine news with entertainment produces not monopolies in the technical sense, but rather intensified competition among corporate superpowers. Indeed, with the centrality of communication satellites at the opening and the climax of *ID4*, the alien Murdoch's acquisition of American citizenship to serve his media expansion in the film's back story and his war with Time-Warner over access to New York City cable television on the horizon (*Variety* would call it 'the clash of the titans'), *Independence Day* is a parable of the battle between global media giants. American victory in that *War of the Worlds*, the message, scores another triumph for the medium, the competition-driven, world-wide consumption of made-in-America culture.[75]

'Motion pictures are the most conspicuous of all American exports. They do not lose their identity. They betray their nationality and country of origin. ... They are demonstrably the greatest single factors in the Americanization of the world and as such fairly may be called the most important and significant of America's exported products.' The 1928 Motion Picture Producers and Distributors Association, speaking for internal consumption and perhaps more frankly than would be typical

today, reminds us of New Hollywood's roots in the classical period.
When the motion picture business sells movies all over the world, it
routinely also markets the goods and services tied into and advertised
within them. *Independence Day*'s 'corporate sponsor', Konica USA, Inc.,
pioneered 'global theatre advertising' by erecting in-theatre displays of a
giant space ship hovering over Times Square. *ID4* uses visual
multiplication and digital technology, just as David uses the computer
virus, to counterpose itself as patriotic motion picture to the alien
invader.[76]

Aliens are imaginary, and no one really gets killed in *Independence
Day*. Exporting virtual rather than actual war, the film-makers see
themselves as meeting the modern hunger not for violence but for myth.
Dean Devlin's mother believed in UFOs; Devlin and Emmerich 'believe
in fantasy' instead. Disavowing the Real Presence of their spiritual vision
is the condition of its promise of solace. But far from offering utopia, a
world elsewhere alternative to the present, *ID4* re-enchants its own
material foundations for the film displays the myth that has governed
military-industrial strategy since World War II. Although the Cold War
featured massive deaths at the peripheries of empire, the distinctive
feature of atomic weapons after Nagasaki was that they could never be
used. These exterminatory instruments, accumulated by both superpowers
at levels that could destroy the planet many times over, were tokens in a
virtual politics of signalling toughness that made permeable the boundary
between military strategy and spectacle. War deaths themselves, derealised
in the foreign policy jargon of demonstration effects, had less to do with
immediate geopolitical objectives than with sending messages to the other
superpower. The end of the Cold War, apparently rendering the virtual
function of military hardware obsolete, threatened to undermine the
entire military-industrial political economy.[77]

The dissolution of a bipolar balance of power has instead spread
virtual war to all areas of military procurement, intensifying the uncanny
mirroring, as symbolic capital, between armaments and entertainment.
Rushing to the defence of aerospace, the 'crown jewel of American
exporters', President Clinton has ended the twenty-year ban on the sale

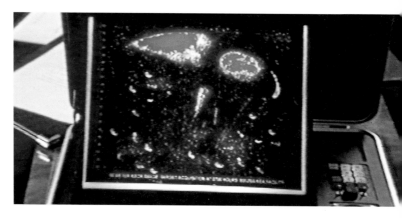

of 'high-performance aircraft and other advanced weapons to Latin America'; pushed for NATO expansion (where, as illustrated by a 'three-day military aviation show' put on in Hungary by mammoth arms manufacturers, 'a need for improved communications systems became a need for the mother of all defense purchases: advanced fighter aircraft' like those used in *ID4*); supported the merger of existing aerospace giants – most recently Boeing and McDonnell Douglas – the better to fit them for global competitition; and budgeted the continued production of billion dollar high-tech instruments of war like the Seawolf submarine which have no foreseeable utility. The Seawolf is, according to its chief petty officer, 'worth every penny. Now if we could only just find somebody to fight with it.' Supplying that enemy tongue-in-cheek, *Independence Day* is the submarine's double, for '[s]tripped of its weapons, the Seawolf is essentially a massive computer stuffed inside a 9,000 ton cigar-shaped tube.' A master of symbolic politics – witness his endorsement of *ID4* – President Clinton supports demonstration grants at all levels of society. But whereas the two thousand families federally subsidised to buy their own homes will set the working poor a good example practically for free, the 2.4 billion dollar Seawolf good example sets the high price of virtual war. Military hardware and software will have their use value again, far from the United States, but *Independence Day* is less significant as propaganda for immediate massive violence than

Human technology tracking alien technology

as military-industrial exchange and symbolic value materialised in popular culture.[78]

And in outer space as well. In a news story with the movie headline, 'Next in Space. Thrills, Chills, Spills,' Clinton is credited with reviving interest in the search for other worlds. The President's proposal that Washington and Moscow join in piloted space exploration, according to the director of space policy at the Federation of Atomic Scientists, was 'the first time the White House had paid close attention to the space program since the moon landings'. The Pathfinder headed for Mars 'largely because human beings hope they are not alone', according to a news story that could have been quoting (from *Contact*) Jodie Foster's extraterrestrial 'vision … that tells us that we are not, that none of us is alone'. *Independence Day* suggests that if '"Loneliness" Drives Our Quest Into Space', fratricide alongside fraternity powers the wish to populate other worlds. The Pathfinder and *ID4* together build support for the $90 billion manned space station, which ministers to American spiritual and military-industrial needs more than any significant scientific purpose. Re-enchanting the long history of the American frontier, NASA named its space ship for the hero of James Fenimore Cooper's Leatherstocking tales, himself baptised for his gun. The space agency directed Pathfinder to land on Mars on 4 July 1997, Independence Day, the first anniversary of the release of the film.[79]

Other 1997 summer blockbusters were also caught up in the *ID4* gravitational pull – the irreverent *Men in Black*, co-starring Will Smith and Tommy Lee Jones as alien hunters (the film's first catch, at the Mexican border, turns out to be an extraterrestrial disguised among illegal aliens; the good alien, masquerading as a Jewish diamond merchant, is killed); the pious *Contact* (a film 'rooted in true scientific believability' according to its director, Robert Zemeckis [*Back to the Future*, *Forrest Gump*], in which Jodie Foster plays a voluntary alien abductee who is visited not by extraterrestrial sexual abuse but by her long-dead father); and three films with White House plots at their centre: *Absolute Power* (the adulterous President is exposed as an accomplice to murder), *Murder at 1600* (the National Security Adviser orchestrates a murder to frame the President's son; Wesley Snipes, playing a black police detective, solves the crime) and *Air Force One* (another endangered Presidential wife and daughter, another former war pilot who gets to fly again; this President, Harrison Ford, foils the hijacking of his plane). Although Clinton is inserted five times into *Contact* to appear to preside over the extraterrestrial mission and endorsed *Air Force One* as a 'terrific movie' (he had taken Harrison Ford on a tour of the aircraft), no 1997 summer blockbuster brought the President together with aliens in a single frame, and none duplicated *ID4*'s success. Like the twelve-foot model that serves as its fifty-mile long mothership, the insubstantial *ID4* casts a long (computer-generated) shadow.[80]

**7** Heaven's Gate

'Murder is a detour on the way to suicide,' in Nietzsche's famous
aphorism. *Independence Day* kills no one, however; it plays with once-
buried unconscious material by licensing itself as fantasy. It briefly
soothes new world disorders without any deep healing of wounds.
Engaging in its own form of plausible deniability, the film wins political
endorsements without taking itself too seriously, flashing across the sky
one long summer but producing no upheavals in its wake. But during the
Easter week nine months after the release of *Independence Day*, in what
the *New York Times* headlined as an 'Eerie Scene Out of Hollywood',
another ending came to pass in southern California. A group calling itself
Heaven's Gate, whose members designed commercial home pages for
the Internet, imagined that 'aliens from space' had 'arrived in staged
spacecraft (UFO) crashes', and 'incarnated' themselves in human bodies.
'UFOs. Why they are here. Who they have come for. When they will
leave,' Heaven's Gate promised to explain. Heaven's Gate took its name
directly from the Bible rather than from Michael Cimino's failed
blockbuster, *Heaven's Gate*. But one of 'at least 100 groups whose
spiritual interest focuses on flying saucers', according to the *Times*,
Heaven's Gate members 'got their ideas about alien spaceships from
Hollywood'.

　　　Like *ID4*, Heaven's Gate inhabited the virtual reality universe of
cyberspace, faith, science fiction and body disturbance. The cult's
founder gave up his 'male companion' and all sexual activity after being
cared for by a hospital nurse; following the lead of one member, who had
the operation performed on alien Mexican soil, he and one-third of his
male followers submitted to castration. Like Russell Casse, those who
belonged to Heaven's Gate believed that space aliens had entered their
bodies. But like *ID4*'s 'biomechanical suits', their bodies were merely
'containers' for their new alien selves. And like the new age Angelenos in
*Independence Day* (and the first victims in *War of the Worlds*), the cultists
believed that the aliens were friendly. The American government was
another story. Worrying that they faced 'some sort of psychological or

physical torture (such as occurred at both Ruby Ridge and Waco)', and imagining that they would be 'picked up' by a UFO spacecraft and flown from the doomed earth to the 'Level Above Human', the members of Heaven's Gate 'exited' their bodies in a mass self-slaughter. They left behind the screenplay for a motion picture of their story; one of its co-authors, who had moved from Heaven's Gate to Beverly Hills and was frightened by the videotapes the cult was sending him, was the man who led police to the bodies.[81]

Like *Independence Day*, Heaven's Gate fleetingly monopolised national attention before disappearing into space. But the apparatus that generated these animistic tales will continue its anthropomorphising work, a culture-machine for the intergalactic global village, reassuring ordinary people that the forces governing the universe and the nation take a human interest. The *Washington Post* reported another death, for example, in the wake of the landing on Mars. 'Suffering from extreme cold', in the *Post*'s words, Pathfinder and its adjunct robot lost contact with earth. 'The pint-size rover Sojourner, like a lost child naively confident of rescue, is probably circling the mothership slowly, clockwise, awaiting a signal that may never come.'[82] America's 'collective unconscious', as Devlin and Emmerich might have put it, was accessing yet another film, *Bambi*.

However popular and poignant the Pathfinder mission – '556 million [Web site] hits in the first thirty days of transmission'[83] – reality

The President confronts the alien threat

constraints deprived it of *Independence Day*'s scope. *Contact*'s alien civilisation beams back to earth the first television transmission: Hitler opening the 1936 Nurenberg Olympic games. When future extraterrestrials pick a comparable single source with which to enlighten the United States about its end-of-the-century past, the prediction here is that they will return the movie that integrates Washington and Hollywood, national history and science fiction, World Wars and Star Wars, secret government and public spectacle, cyberspace and outer space, aliens and aliens, Jews and blacks, motherships and prayer, nuclear destruction and AIDS, military procurement and family entertainment, the movie that brings it all back home.

# Notes

**1** Independence Day, dir. Roland Emmerich (Twentieth Century Fox, 1996); 'Declaration of Independence', *Starburst Yearbook*, 1996–97, p. 62; Maria La Ganga, 'Dole on Research Mission to the Movies', *Los Angeles Times*, 30 July 1996, p. A19; Richard Corliss, 'The Invasion Has Begun!' *Time*, 8 July 1996, pp. 58–9.

**2** John Sutherland, 'Ghosts in the Wind Machine', *TLS*, 5 July 1996, p. 17; David E. Williams, 'Worlds at War', *American Cinematographer*, July 1996, pp. 32–3; Louise McElvague, 'Producers Find Hollywood News a Big Story Overseas', *Los Angeles Times*, 8 March, 1996, p. D4; Chris Petrikin, 'Canvick Confab Gets H.W.D film Commissioners the Inside Scoop', *Variety*, 30 September, 1996, p. 7. The third city to suffer initial annihilation was New York, the financial leg of the imperial American tripod.

**3** Maria La Ganga, 'Dole II Offers Praise for Hollywood', and 'Dole on Research Mission to the Movies', *Los Angeles Times*, 31 July 1996, p. A14; 30 July 1996, p. A19; Bernard Weinraub, 'Films and Records Threaten Social Fabric, Dole Asserts', *New York Times*, 1 June 1995, pp. A1, B10. The referenced films are *The Birth of a Nation*, dir. D.W. Griffith (Epoch, 1915); *Gone with the Wind*, dir. Victor Fleming (MGM, 1939); Patton, dir. Francis Ford Coppola (Twentieth Century Fox, 1970); *Natural Born Killers*, dir. Oliver Stone (Warner Bros., 1994); *Striptease*, dir. Andrew Bergman (Castle Rock, 1996).

**4** Adam Nagourney, 'Public Endorses Uplifting Movies, Dole Tells Hollywood', *New York Times*, 31 July 1996, p. B7; William J. Bennett, *The Book of Virtues: A Treasury of Great Moral Stories* (New York: Simon and Schuster, 1993); William J. Bennett and C. DeLores Tucker, 'Smut-Free Stores', *New York Times*, 9 December 1996, p. A15.

**5** *New York Times*, 31 July 1996, p. B7; *Time*, 8 July 1996, p. 64; James Wolcott, 'Reborn on the Fourth of July', *New Yorker*, 17 July 1996, p. 80; *Independence Day* advertisement, *New York Times*, 2 July 1996, p. C13; *Time*, 'Aliens Have Landed!' 8 July 1996, cover, pp. 58–62; *Newsweek*, 'Out There', 8 July 1996 cover, pp. 48–54, 57.

**6** Carol Diuguid, 'Crix' Voices Echo Public Vote at B.O.', *Variety*, 13–19 January 1997, p. 12; Bernard Weinraub, 'Films Vault to the Top with Tricks, Not Stars', *New York Times*, 9 July 1996, p. C11; Janet Maslin, 'Space Aliens, Action and a Chance to Save the Planet', *New York Times*, 2 July 1996, pp. C11, C18; 'Variety Box Office', and Leonard Klady, '"Day" Breaks with Record B.O. Takings', *Variety*, 15–21 July 1996, p. 16; *Variety*, 'EDI Box Office News', 23 December 1996–5; January 1997, p. 20; *Variety*, 'Top 20 Grossers of '96', 6–12 January 1997, p. 10. Adjusting revenues to account for inflation and ticket-price rises, *Independence Day* falls to thirty-second. *Gone with the Wind* remains in first place. See 'Gross Adjustments', *Variety*, 28 October–3 November 1996, p. 16.

**7** New York Times, 30 July 1996, p. B7; *Forrest Gump*, dir. Robert Zemeckis (Paramount, 1994). As of this writing, *Forrest Gump* and *Independence Day* are in fourth and seventh place among top-grossing movies. See Movieweb, 'Top 50 All Time Highest Grossing Movies', <http:www.movieweb.com/movie/alltime.html>, 7 August 1997.

**8** Cuomo is quoted in Marilyn D. Young, 'Dangerous History: Vietnam and the "Good War"', in Edward T. Linenthal and Tom Engelhardt (eds), *History Wars: The Enola*

*Gay and other Battles for the American Past* (New York, 1996), pp. 203–4. On *ID4*'s digital technology, see Bruce Newman, 'Computers Now, Apocalpyse Coming Right Up', *New York Times*, 30 June 1996, p. H11; Williams, 'Worlds at War', pp. 32–47; Tim Prokop, 'Fireworks', *Cineflex* vol. 67, September 1996, pp. 61–85.

**9** Jonathan Romney, 'Terminated', *The Guardian*, 21 December 1996, p. 6; Caryn James, 'Giant Flying Saucers! Better Run and Hide', *New York Times*, 21 July 1996, p. H9; Louis Menand, 'Hollywood's Trap', *New York Review of Books*, 19 September 1996, p. 6.

**10** David Denby, 'Apocalypse, Wow!', *New York*, 8 July 1996, p. 47; *Time*, 8 July 1996, p. 60; *New York Times*, 9 July 1996, p. C11; 31 July 1996, p. B7; Roald Rynning, 'The American President', *Films in Review*, vol. 47, September/October 1996, pp. 70–1; Los Angeles Times, 30 July 1996, p. A19; Mary Bruno (ed.), 'Mr. ShowBiz News Archive', '*Happy Independence Day*', <http://www.mrshowbiz.com>, 4 July 1996; *Schindler's List*, dir. Steven Spielberg (Amblin Entertainment, 1993).

**11** *Sands of Iwo Jima*, dir. Allan Dwan (Republic, 1949).

**12** Doris Kearns Goodwin, *No Ordinary Time. Franklin and Eleanor Roosevelt: The Home Front in World War II* (New York: Simon and Schuster, 1994); Michael Rogin, 'The President, the cousin he was having an affair with, the cousin he was married to, and her girlfriend', *London Review of Books*, 21 September 1995, pp. 7–9.

**13** On *Schindler's List* and its reception, see Miriam Hansen, '*Schindler's List* Is Not *Shoah*: The Second Commandment, Popular Modernism, and Public Memory', *Critical Inquiry* vol. 22, Winter 1996, pp. 292–312.

**14** The quotes in the text are from John W. Dower, 'Three Narratives of Our Humanity',

and Tom Engelhardt, 'The Victors and the Vanquished', in Linenthal and Engelhardt (eds), *History Wars*, pp. 72–3, 244. I have drawn on several articles from this volume for the analysis in this and subsequent paragraphs.

**15** Paul Boyer, *By the Bomb's Early Light: American Thought and Culture at the Dawn of the Atomic Age* (New York: Pantheon, 1985), pp. 7–8; Edward T. Linenthal, 'Anatomy of a Controversy', in Linenthal and Engelhardt (eds), *History Wars*, pp. 13–14; Tom Engelhardt, *The End of Victory Culture: Cold War America and the Disillusioning of a Generation* (New York: Basic Books, 1995).

**16** Dower, 'Three Narratives', pp. 75, 93–5; Boyer, *Bomb's Early Light*, p. 213. As Lon Troyer has pointed out to me, the controversy in the year following the release of *ID4* over the giant size and invasive mall placement of the proposed World War II memorial, between the Washington Monument and the Lincoln Memorial, also attested to World War II's awkward presence in the American imagination.

**17** Boyer, *Bomb's Early Light*, pp. 14, 67.

**18** Dower, 'Three Narratives', Mike Wallace, 'Culture Wars, History Front', in Linenthal and Engelhardt, *History Wars*, pp. 75, 171–98.

**19** Wallace, 'Culture Wars', p. 185. The lone dissenter thought the condemnation was insufficiently strong.

**20** Engelhardt, 'Victors and Vanquished', p. 248; Tom Engelhardt, 'Plugging Culture', *The Nation*, 8/15 September 1997, p. 27.

**21** *Back to the Future*, dir. Robert Zemeckis (Universal/Amblin, 1985); Robin Wood, *Hollywood from Vietnam to Reagan* (New York: Columbia University Press, 1986). See also Andrew Britton, 'Blissing Out: The Politics of Reaganite Entertainment', *Movie* vol. 31/32, Winter 1986, pp. 1–42. The films made between 1965 and 1976 that are named in the text are *Bonnie and Clyde*, dir.

Arthur Penn (Seven Arts, 1967); *Easy Rider*, dir. Dennis Hopper (Columbia, 1969); *Medium Cool*, dir. Haskell Wexler (Paramount, 1969); *Nashville*, dir. Robert Altman (Paramount, 1975); *Taxi Driver*, dir. Martin Scorsese (Columbia, 1976). It would be easy to compile a much longer list, including movies varying widely in quality and popularity, for example including *The Chase*, dir. Arthur Penn (Columbia, 1966); *In the Heat of the Night*, dir. Norman Jewison (United Artists, 1967); *The Graduate*, dir. Mike Nichols (Embassy Pictures, 1968); *Zabriskie Point*, dir. Michelangelo Antonioni (MGM, 1970); *Chinatown*, dir. Roman Polanski (Paramount, 1974); *Missouri Breaks*, dir. Arthur Penn (United Artists, 1976); and perhaps ending with *Apocalypse Now*, dir. Francis Ford Coppola (Zeotrope, 1979). Theodore Draper, *A Very Thin Line: The Iran – Contra Affair* (New York: Hill and Wang, 1991) pp. 558–63.

**22** Thomas Schatz, 'The New Hollywood', *Film Theory Goes to the Movies*, ed. Jim Collins, Hilary Radner and Ava Preacher Collins (New York: Routledge, 1993), pp. 8–36 (quoted p. 9); Scott Bukatman, *Blade Runner* (London: British Film Institute, 1997), p. 16. As of the end of 1996, all six films in the *Star Wars* trilogy (1977–83) and the *Indiana Jones* trilogy (1981–9) remained among the top thirty all-time domestic grossers. Using the measure of film rentals, the money returned to distributors, the *Star Wars* and *Indiana Jones* trilogies were in the all-time top twenty. *E.T.* was first, *Independence Day* fifth, *Forrest Gump* seventh and *Jaws* thirteenth. Before the re-release of *Star Wars*, the New Hollywood's top success was *E.T.: The Extra-Terrestrial*, dir. Steven Spielberg (Universal, 1982), the future maker of *Schindler's List. Star Wars* and *E.T.* are now in third and fourth place among adjusted domestic grossers, after

*Gone with the Wind* and *Snow White*. The New Hollywood, beginning with *Jaws*, has produced only twelve of the top thirty-two all-time adjusted top grossers. *Independence Day* is among them. Box office figures are from *Variety*, 28 October–3 November 1996, p. 16 and Movienews, 'Top 50 All Time Highest Grossing Movies'. Additional film references are *Star Wars*, dir. George Lucas (Lucasfilm, 1977); *The Empire Strikes Back*, dir. George Lucas (Lucasfilm, 1980); *The Return of the Jedi*, dir. George Lucas (Lucasfilm, 1983); *Indiana Jones*, dir. Steven Spielberg (Lucasfilm/ Paramount, 1981); *Indiana Jones and the Temple of Doom*, dir. Steven Spielberg (Lucasfilm/ Paramount, 1984); *Indiana Jones and the Last Command,* dir. Steven Spielberg (Lucasfilm/ Paramount, 1989); *Snow White* (Walt Disney, 1937); *Fantasia* (Walt Disney, 1940); *Bambi* (Walt Disney, 1942); *Cinderella* (Walt Disney, 1950); *Jaws*, dir. Steven Spielberg (MCA/Universal, 1975).

**23** Michael Rogin, *'Ronald Reagan', the Movie and other Episodes in Political Demonology* (Berkeley: University of California Press, 1987), pp. 1–43; Garry Wills, *Reagan's America: Innocents at Home* (Garden City: Doubleday, 1987); *Murder in the Air*, dir. Lewis Seiler (Warner Bros., 1940).

**24** 'Houston, We Have a Big Problem', *Empire*, September 1996, p. 120; 'Declaration of Independence', *Starburst* Yearbook 1996–7, pp. 63–4.

**25** I am indebted to Kathleen Moran's comments on an earlier draft of this essay, and to her unpublished paper, 'The New Cinema of Attractions'.

**26** The classic source on the cinema of attractions is Tom Gunning, 'The Cinema of Attractions: Early Film, Its Spectator, and the Avant-Garde', *Early Cinema: Space, Frame, Narrative*, ed. Thomas Elsaesser (London: British Film Institute, 1990), pp. 56–62. Film references are *Rambo: First Blood*, dir. Ted Kotcheff (Carolco, 1982); *Rambo: First Blood Part II*, dir. George P. Cosmatos (Tristar, 1985); *The Terminator*, dir. James Cameron (Cinema 84/Pacific Western, 1984); *Pulp Fiction*, dir. Quentin Tarantino (Miramax, 1994).

**27** Fredric Jameson, *The Political Unconscious: Narrative as a Socially Symbolic Act* (Ithaca: Cornell University Press, 1981).

**28** Boyer, *Bomb's Early Light*, pp. 7, 16; Romney, 'Terminated', p. 6; Leo Charney, paper on 1970s disaster films delivered at the University of California, Berkeley, 17 March 1997. The 'age of anxiety' was W.H. Auden's widely-adopted term for the 1950s. Film references are *Invaders from Mars*, dir. William Cameron Menzies (National, 1953); *War of the Worlds*, dir. Byron Haskin (Paramount, 1953); *Airport*, dir. George Seaton (Universal, 1970).

**29** *New York Times*, 30 June 1996, p. H11; Romney, 'Terminated', p. 6; Robert Bresson, *Notes on the Cinematographer*, transl. Jonathan Griffin (London: Quartet Books, 1986), p. 69; Ann Banfield, 'L'Imparfait de l'objectif: The Imperfect of the Object Glass', *Camera Obscura* vol. 24, September 1990, pp. 65–87 (Bresson quoted p. 65); Charney, UC Berkeley lecture; *JFK*, dir. Oliver Stone (Warner Bros., 1991); Gunning, 'Cinema of Attractions', pp. 56–62.

**30** Alan D. Sokal, 'Transgressing the Boundaries: Toward a Tranformational Hermeneutics of Quantum Gravity', *Social Text* vol. 46–7, Spring/Summer 1996, pp. 217–52; Janny Scott, 'Postmodern Gravity Deconstructed, Slyly', *New York Times*, 18 May 1996, pp. 1, 22; Richard Lewontin, 'Billions and Billions of Demons', *New York Review of Books*, 9 January 1997, pp. 28–31 (majority belief in UFOs, p. 28); Adam Rogers and T. Trent Gegax, 'Alien Invasion!' *Newsweek*, 8 July 1996, p. 50; Amy Harmon, 'UFOs: Believing Without Seeing', *International Herald Tribune*, 16 June 1997, p. 2.

**31** *Them!*, dir. Gordon Douglas (Warner Bros., 1954).

**32** *Time*, 8 July 1996, p. 60; *Newsweek*, 8 July 1996, p. 50; Bruce Handy, 'Roswell or Bust', *Time*, 23 June 1997, pp. 64–5; Leon Jaroff, 'Did Aliens Really Land?' *Time*, 23 June 1997, p. 68; *Time*, 'The Roswell Files', 23 June 1997, cover, pp. 62–71; Harmon, 'UFOs', p. 2; 'Inside *Independence Day*', <http:www.ddc.com>, 5 July 1997.

**33** *Time*, 8 July 1996, p. 60; *Newsweek*, 8 July 1996, p. 50; Handy, 'Roswell or Bust', p. 66; Harmon, 'UFOs', p. 2.

**34** Harmon, 'UFOs', p. 2; '"Space Aliens"? No, Just Dummies', *International Herald Tribune*, 25 June 1997, p. 3; Jaroff, 'Did Aliens Really Land?' p. 71; William J. Broad, 'Military Lied About Nature of UFOs, CIA Reports', *International Herald Tribune*, 4 August 1997, p. 3; Handy, 'Roswell or Bust', p. 66; David Wise, 'When the Lies Come from Above', *International Herald Tribune*, 9–10 August 1997, p. 6.

**35** Handley, 'Roswell or Bust', p. 65; Barry Hillenbrand, 'Celebration of Hope', *Time*, 11 December 1995, p. 62; James Bowman, 'Let Me Entertain You', *American Spectator*, September 1996, p. 68.

**36** Matthew J. Wald, 'Atomic Tests from '51 to '68 Threatened Millions of Children, Study Says', *International Herald Tribune*, 30 July 1997, p. 3; Robert Cantwell, *When We Were Good: The Folk Revival* (Cambridge: Harvard University Press, 1996), pp. 183, 170. See also Michael S. Sherry, *In the Shadow of War: The United States since the 1930s* (New Haven: Yale University Press, 1995).

**37** I saw Severen Darden do his Newton/Mars routine at Chicago's Second City, *circa* 1960.

**38** *New York Times Magazine*, 'Antipolitics '94', 16 October 1994, p. 37, quoted in Jodi

Dean, 'Coming Out as an Alien: Feminists, UFOs, and the "Oprah Effect"', in Nan Bauer Maglin and Donna Perry (eds), *'Bad Girls' 'Good Girls': Women, Sex, and Power in the Nineties* (New Brunswick: Rutgers University Press, 1996), p. 92.

**39** It should be noted, however, that the majority of eligible Americans failed to vote at all in 1996, matching the smallest turnout in a US Presidential election in almost two centuries, and that elites are feeling better than the population as a whole. Whereas the percentage of opinion leaders satisfied with conditions in the United States jumped in four years from 25–73%, the shift among the public is from 20–45%. See Steven Erlanger, 'U.S. Role in World? Gap in Views', *International Herald Tribune*,11–12 October 1997, p. 3; Walter Dean Burnham, 'Bill Clinton: Riding the Tiger', in Gerald M. Pomper (ed.), *The Election of 1996: Reports and Interpretations* (Chatham, New Jersey: Chatham House, 1997), pp. 1–20. Thanks to Lon Troyer for suggesting the relevance of *The Day the Earth Stood Still*, dir. Robert Wise (Twentieth Century Fox, 1951). For the 'FBI assault' on the Waco compound see Pierre Thomas, 'Reno "Seriously Negligent" in Waco', *Washington Post*, 12 July 1996, A21.

**40** Judith Miller, 'Making Money Abroad, and Also a Few Enemies', *New York Times*, 26 January 1997, p. A11. Conversely, when *Independence Day* gives offence, it does so as a politically correct film, as in *Positif*, October 1996, p. 45: 'La niaserie du scénario n'a d'égale que sa valeur symbolique et sociologique, dans sa culture du politiquement correct.' ('The inanity of the screenplay is only matched by its symbolic and sociological value in the culture of political correctness.')

**41** Arthur Schlesinger, Jr., *The Disuniting of America: Reflections on a Multicultural*

*Society* (New York: Norton, 1991), pp. 118–20.

**42** Schlesinger, *Disuniting of America*, pp. 119, 131 (quoting Fuchs); Peter Brimelaw, *Alien Nation: Common Sense About America's Immigration Disaster* (New York: Harper Collins, 1995); Thomas Byrne and Mary Bird Edsall, *Chain Reaction: The Impact of Race, Rights, and Taxes on American Politics* (New York: Norton, 1992).

**43** Compare Michael Rogin, *Blackface, White Noise: Jewish Immigrants in the Hollywood Melting Pot* (Berkeley: University of California Press, 1996) and Paul Berman, 'The Other and the Almost the Same', in Berman (ed.), *Blacks and Jews: Alliances and Arguments* (New York: Delacorte Press, 1994), pp. 1–28. See also Donna Rosenthal, 'Did Cultures Clash over "Schindler's"?' *Los Angeles Times*, 22 January 1994, pp. F1, F9; Donna Rosenthal, 'Spielberg Hailed, Wilson Chided at Oakland School', *New York Times*, 12 April 1994, p. A3; *New York Times*, 'Laughter at Film Brings Spielberg Visit', 13 April 1994, p. B11.

**44** Benjamin Demott, *The Trouble with Friendship: Why Americans Can't Think Straight about Race* (New York: Atlantic Monthly Press, 1995); *Los Angeles Times*, 30 July 1996, p. A19; *Deep Cover*, dir. Bill Duke (New Line Cinema, 1992); *The Great White Hype*, dir. Reginald Hudlin (Twentieth Century Fox, 1996).

**45** Frances Fitzgerald, *America Revised: History Schoolbooks in the Twentieth Century* (Boston: Little, Brown, 1979), p. 93; Michael Rogin, 'The Two Declarations of American Independence', and Reva B. Siegel, 'The Racial Rhetoric of Colorblind Constitutionalism: The Case of *Hopwood v. Texas*', in Robert Post and Michael Rogin (eds), *Race and Representation: Affirmative Action* (New York: Zone Books, 1998); D.H. Lawrence, *Studies in Classic American*

*Literature* (New York: Viking, 1964 [1923]); Leslie Fiedler, *Love and Death in the American Novel* (New York: Stein and Day, 1960).

**46** Wolcott, 'Reborn on the Fourth of July', p. 80; Cornel West and Michael Lerner, *Let the Healing Begin* (New York: Putnam's, 1995); Rogin, *Blackface, White Noise*, pp. 81–102, 170; *The Jazz Singer*, Alan Crosland dir. (Warner Bros., 1927).

**47** Jewish Communication Network Forum: David Notowitz on Jewish film-making, <http://www. jcn18.com>, 23 December 1996–14 January 1997; Carrie Goringe, Nitrate Online Review, '*Independence Day*', <http://www.nitrateonline.com>, 5 July 1997; Kenneth Turan, 'The Day the Script Stood Still', <http//www .hollywood.com>, 2 July 1997; Maslin, 'Space Aliens', pp. C11, C18; Herbert Gans, 'Symbolic Ethnicity: the Future of Ethnic Groups and Cultures in America', *Ethnic and Racial Studies* vol. 2, January 1979, pp. 1–20; Richard Alba, *Ethnic Identity: The Transformation of Ethnic Identity in White America* (New Haven: Yale University Press, 1990), quoted pp. 306, 318.

**48** Patricia Erens, *The Jew in American Cinema* (Bloomington, Indiana: Indiana University Press, 1984); Movieweb, 'Top Fifty All Time Highest Grossers'; *Jurassic Park*, dir. Steven Spielberg (MCA/Universal, 1993); *The Lost World: Jurassic Park*, dir. Steven Spielberg (MCA/Universal, 1997).

**49** 'The Director: Roland Who?' *Sight and Sound* supplement, September 1996, p. 13; *Dr. Strangelove, Or How I Learned to Stop Worrying and Love the Bomb* dir. Stanley Kubrick (Columbia, 1963); Zbigniew Brzezinski, *Between Two Ages: America's Role in the Technetronic Era* (New York: Viking, 1970). Thanks to Masha Raskolnikov for recognising Nimziki as Brzezinski.

**50** Homer Harris, 'Atomic Bomb Blues', *News and the Blues*, Columbia CT46217;

Michael Crichton, *Rising Sun: A Novel* (New York: Knopf, 1992); *The Rising Sun*, dir. Philip Kaufman (Twentieth Century Fox, 1993). Even in the mood of American triumphalism that has succeeded *ID4*, the felt Asian threat has not so much dissipated as shifted from Japan to China – an ominous presence in the global political economy, in American elections and (in the persons of disproportionately qualified Asian-Americans) in college admissions.

**51** Don Pease, comments at Englisches Seminar workshop, Universität zu Köln.

**52** *Chicago Hope*, CBS, 5 February 1996; Hollywood Online, 'Margaret Colin (Constance)',<http://www.hollywood.com>. Peter Emonds-Banfield reports (in personal conversation) an *X Files* episode that also capitalises on the alien/aliens and alien/goverment double entendres: after Mexican field workers are infected by a strange combination pesticide and virus (on the virus, see below), an old woman reports that extraterrestrials have taken her daughter away. The black helicopters turn out to belong, however, to the infectious disease unit of the US government.

**53** *New York Times*, 4 July 1996, p. C17. Alien hostage-takers serve as stand-ins for Middle Eastern terrorists in the 1986 film, *Aliens*. See Melani McAlister, *Staging the American Century: Race, Gender, and Nation in U.S. Representations of the Middle East, 1945-1992* (Berkeley and Los Angeles: University of California Press, forthcoming), mss. Chapter 5, pp. 258–61.

**54** Sigmund Freud, 'Psycho-Analytic Notes on an Autobiographical Account of a Case of Paranoia (Dementia Paranoides)', in *Standard Edition of the Complete Psychological Works of Sigmund Freud*, ed. James Strachey, 24 vols (London: Hogarth Press, 1953–74), vol. 12, pp. 3–79; Darden, Second City, *circa* 1960; Jeffrey Klein,

'Nativist Son', *Mother Jones*, November–December, 1993, p. 3; Paul Glastris, 'Immigration Boomerang', *U.S. News and World Report*, 17 March, 1977, pp. 24–6.

**55** Laura Mulvey, *Fetishism and Curiousity* (Bloomington, Indiana: Indiana University Press, 1996), p. 121.

**56** Colgate dental cream advertisement, *Life*, 20 December 1954, p. 8; 31 January 1955, p. 40; Susan Jeffords, *Hard Bodies: Hollywood Masculinity in the Reagan Era* (New Brunswick, New Jersey: Rutgers University Press, 1994); Klaus Theweleit, *Male Fantasies, Volume 2. Male Bodies: Psychoanalyzing the White Terror*, trans. Erica Carter and Chris Turner (Minneapolis: University of Minnesota Press, 1989), pp. 210–25; James William Gibson, *Warrior Dreams: Paramilitary Culture in Post-Vietnam America* (New York: Hill and Wang, 1994); Rogin, *'Ronald Reagan', the Movie*, pp. 1–3, 43.

**57** Mr Showbiz Star Bios, 'Brent Spiner', <http://www. mrshowbiz.com>, 5 July 1997; Donna Haraway, 'A Cyborg Manifesto', in *Simians, Cyborgs, and Women: The Reinvention of Nature* (New York: Routledge, 1991), pp. 149–82.

**58** *2001: A Space Odyssey*, dir. Stanley Kubrick (MGM, 1968).

**59** Simon Bacal, *'Independence Day* Special FX', *Starburst* vol. 217, September 1996, p. 17; *Everything You Always Wanted to Know about Sex*, dir. Woody Allen (United Artists, 1972); *Alien*, dir. Ridley Scott (Twentieth Century Fox, 1978); Barbara Creed, *The Monstrous Feminine: Film, Feminism, Psychoanalysis* (London: Routledge, 1993), pp. 16–19.

**60** Gorringe, *'Independence Day'*; Sarah Kerr, 'Fetal Attraction: Will Robert Zemeckis Never Grow Up?' <http://www.slate.com>, 11 July 1997; *Close Encounters of the Third Kind*, dir.

Steven Spielberg (Columbia, 1977); *Fatal Attraction*, dir. Adrian Lyne (Paramount, 1987).

**61** Creed, *Monstrous Feminine*, pp. 5–7, *passim*; Engelhardt, 'Victors and Vanquished', and Linenthal, 'Anatomy of a Controversy', in *History Wars*, pp. 230–1, 12; Michael Rogin, '"Kiss Me Deadly": Communism, Motherhood, and Cold War Movies', in *'Ronald Reagan,' the Movie*, pp. 242–4, 263–7; Hollywood Online Video Guide, *Independence Day*, <http://www.hollywood.com>; Williams, 'Worlds at War', p. 32.

**62** Robin Marantz Henig, 'Viruses: What We Know', *Vogue*, March 1988, p. 326, quoted in Jill Hargis, 'Body Piercing: Positioning the Self in the Psyche and the Social', seminar paper, University of California, Berkeley, 1996.

**63** Henig, 'Viruses: What We Know', p. 326; Peter Jaret, 'Our Immune System: The Wars Within', *National Geographic*, June 1986, pp. 702–3; Cindy Patton, *Inventing AIDS* (New York: Routledge, 1990), pp. 59–60, 150.

**64** Haraway is cited in Paula A. Treichler, 'AIDS, Homophobia, and Biomedical Disease: An Epidemic of Signification', in Douglas Crimp (ed.), *AIDS: Cultural Analysis, Cultural Activism* (Cambridge: MIT Press, 1988), p. 59; Richard Rorty and Winifred Rauschenbush are quoted on 'the Communist virus' in Rogin, *Blackface, White Noise*, p. 260.

**65** Compare Cantwell, *When We Were Good*, p. 160, and Michel Foucault, *The History of Sexuality, Vol. 1* (New York: Vintage, 1980), p. 137:
Wars are no longer waged in the name of a sovereign who must be defended; they are waged on behalf of the existence of everyone; entire populations are mobilized for the purpose of wholesale slaughter in the name of life necessity. … [A]s the technology of wars has caused them to tend increasingly toward all-out destruction, the decision that

initiates them [is] … increasingly informed by the naked question of survival.
(Thanks to Lon Troyer for this citation.)

**66** *Invasion of the Body Snatchers*, dir. Don Siegel (Walter Wanger/Allied Arts, 1956); *Time*, 8 July 1996, p. 62; Treichler, 'AIDS, Homophobia', pp. 59–60; Jaret, 'Our Immune System', pp. 702, 710, 723–24; Patton, *Inventing AIDS*, pp. 90–2, 116–18; Sander L. Gilman, 'AIDS and Syphilis: The Iconography of Disease', in *AIDS: Cultural Analysis, Cultural Activism*, pp. 100–3. Compare Richard Price, *Clockers* (New York: Avon, 1992), p. 229: '"You ever see *War of the Worlds*?" Rocco asked Dolan. "No one can stop the Martians and they're blasting the shit out of everybody. You remember what finally killed them?" "The Virus?" Dolan asked.' 'The Virus' is the street name for AIDS.

**67** Harvey Feirstein website, <http://www.plump.com>; 'The Remington Review', <http://wwwa.com/rem>, 5 July 1997; <http://www.music.sony.com/Music/Artist/Info/HarryConnickJr_She.html,1.24>; Mr Showbiz Star Bios, 'Will Smith', http://www. mrshowbiz.com>, 5 July 1997; Fiedler, *Love and Death in the American Novel*; Eric Lott, *Love and Theft: Blackface Minstrelsy and the Working Class* (New York: Oxford University Press, 1993).

**68** *Stargate*, dir. Roland Emmerich (Canal +/Centropolis, 1994); *The Crying Game*, dir. Neal Jordan (Channel 4, 1992). Thanks to Alyson Cole for calling attention to what Harry Connick, Jr. and Jaye Davidson brought to *Independence Day*.

**69** That orifice, beaming its light down on Will Smith, is *Time*'s *ID4* cover; *Newsweek* chose an alien.

**70** Dean, 'Coming Out as an Alien', pp. 92–4. Sexualising atomic warfare, *ID4* may also be alluding to the opening of *Strangelove*, which shows one plane

refuelling another in mid-air. That scene itself is a quote from Josef von Sternberg's *Jet Pilot* (Universal, 1957).

**71** Carol Clover, *Men, Women, and Chain Saws: Gender in the Modern Horror Film* (Princeton: Princeton University Press, 1992), pp. 65–113, quoted p. 80.

**72** Sigmund Freud, 'The Most Prevalent Form of Degradation in Erotic Life', in *Sexuality and the Psychology of Love*, ed. Philip Rieff (New York: Collier, 1963 [1912]), p. 69, and 'From the History of an Infantile Neurosis', in *Three Case Histories*, ed. Philip Rieff (New York: Collier, 1963 [1918], pp. 161–280; Jesse Berrett, 'The Secret Lives of Consumer Culture', unpublished Ph.D. dissertation, University of California, Berkeley, 1996, pp. 296–7; Creed, *Monstrous Feminine*, p. 162; Rogin, '"Kiss Me Deadly"', pp. 241–5, 250–3; Lee Edelman, 'Seeing Things: Representation, the Scene of Surveillance, and the Spectacle of Gay Male Sex', and David Miller, 'Anal Rope', in Diana Fuss (ed.), *Inside/Out: Lesbian Theories, Gay Theories* (New York: Routledge, 1991), pp. 93–141; Leo Bersani, 'Is the Rectum a Grave?' in Crimp (ed.), *AIDS: Cultural Analysis, Cultural Activism*.

**73** Procop, 'Fireworks', p. 84; Hollywood Online, 'Randy Quaid (Russell)',<http:www.hollywood.com>.

**74** Michael Rogin, 'The King's Two Bodies: Lincoln, Wilson, Nixon, and Presidential Self-Sacrifice', in *'Ronald Reagan,' the Movie*, pp. 104–5; Wolcott, 'Reborn on the Fourth of July', p. 80.

**75** V. Vale and Andrea Juno, 'Introduction', in Vale and Juno (eds), *Re/search in Modern Primitives: An Investigation of Contemporary Adornment and Ritual* (San Francisco: V/Search Publications, 1989), p. 5, quoted in Hargis, 'Body Piercing'; *Time*, 8 July 1996, p. 64; *New York Times*, 1 June 1995, p. A1; Mark Crispin Miller, 'Free the Media', and

'The National Enfotainment State', *Nation*, vol. 262, 3 June 1996, pp. 9–15, 23–7; Petrikin, 'Canuck Confab', p. 7. Thanks to Jerry Christiansen for *ID4* as media war. Mass media danger served as both message and medium in Orson Welles's 1938 radio broadcast of *The War of the Worlds*, which a panicked population took for a real invasion, and whose notoriety served as a model for *Independence Day*'s pre-release advertising campaign. See 'Declaration of Independence', *Starburst Yearbook*, p. 61; Michael Denning, *The Cultural Front: The Laboring of American Culture in the Twentieth Century* (London: Verso, 1996), pp. 382–3.

**76** Ruth Vasey, *The World According to Hollywood* (Madison: University of Wisconsin Press, 1997), p. 43; 'Konica USA., Inc Becomes First Corporation Featured in Theater Advertising for a Major Studio Film Release', <http://www.konica.com>, 5 July 1997.

**77** *Sight and Sound* supplement, 'Making a Movie and Making Money: *Independence Day*', September 1996, pp. 12–13; Jonathan Schell, *The Time of Illusion* (New York: Knopf, 1975), and *The Fate of the Earth* (New York: Knopf,1982).

**78** Jeff Gerth, 'Business Gains with Democrats', *New York Times*, 26 December, 1996, p. B7; 'Clinton Ends Latin American Arms Ban', *International Herald Tribune*, 2 August 1997, p. 1; Bill Mesler, 'NATO's New Arms Bazaar', *The Nation*, 21 July 1997, pp. 24, 26; John Mintz, 'Costly New U.S. Sub Has a Mission: Fighting the Budget Battle', *International Herald Tribune*, 21 July 1997, p. 3; Louis Menand, 'Inside the Billway', *New York Review of Books*, 14 August 1997, p. 4.

**79** Dale Bumpers, 'Supporting Mir is Money Lost in Space', *New York Times*, 2 September 1997, p. A20; William J. Broad, 'Next in Space. Thrills, Chills, Spills', John Noble Wilford, 'A Hopeful Cosmic Search: "Loneliness" Drives Our Quest Into Space', 'Beep! U.S. Spacecraft Bounces Down Safely on Mars', *International Herald Tribune,* 21 July 1997, p. 105–6 July 1997, p. 1, 5–6 July 1997, pp. 1, 6. Wilford's story appeared simultaneously with the 5 July preview release of *Contact* (dir. Robert Zemeckis [Warner Bros., 1997]).

**80** Wilford, 'A Hopeful Cosmic Search', p. 1; Handy, 'Roswell or Bust', p. 65; *Men in Black*, dir. Barry Sonnenfeld (MacDonald-Parkes/ Columbia/Amblin, 1997); *Absolute Power*, dir. Clint Eastwood (Castle Rock, 1997); *Murder at 1600*, dir. Dwight H. Little (Warner Bros., 1997); *Air Force One*, dir. Wolfgang Petersen (Beacon Pictures/ Radiant Products/Columbia, 1997); Stephen Hunter, '"Air Force One": Pressurized Ride', *Washington Post*, 25 July, 1997, pp. B1, B6; Phiip Stenon, 'What's Wrong with This Picture of Women in the Military?' *New York Times*, 31 August 1997; Bernard Weinraub, 'Now at a Theater Near You: That Disappointing Season', *New York Times*, 2 September 1997, p. C11; Prokop, 'Fireworks', p. 65.

The most successful of the 1997 films, *Men in Black*, which followed *ID4* as the top US grosser of 1997, is now placed twelfth on the all-time list ('Top Grossing Movies of All-Time', 16 October 1997, <http:/www.excalibur.com/seaquest.topgros. htm>). As for *Contact*, which is dedicated 'to Carl' (the astronomer Carl Sagan who served as 'co-producer' and died during the filming), it is based on Sagan's *Contact: A Novel* (New York: Simon and Shuster, 1985). But Sagan also authored the defence of science against magical causal thinking, *The Demon-Haunted World: Science as a Candle in the Dark* (New York: Simon and Shuster, 1995), that occasioned Richard Lowentin's 'Billions and Billions of Demons' (see Note 30).

1997 ended with *Alien Resurrection*, dir. Jean-Pierre Jeunet (Twentieth Century Fox, 1997), which features alien and full-sized deformed human foetuses, a biologically-engineered queen alien who reproduces without a human host, and contaminated blood that destroys whatever it touches. The film opens with a monstrous birth from Ripley's (Sigourney Weaver's) chest; it ends when Ripley, 'the monster's mother', opens a hole in the space ship, Betty, through which the alien is sucked out in an after-birth abortion. Betty's name and logo pay homage to the favourite GI pin-up of World War II, Betty Grable, whose presence on plane fuselages anticipated the sobriquet, Enola Gay.

**81** Friedrich Nietzsche, Aphorism 338, *The Gay Science*; Todd S. Purdom, 'Tapes Left by 39 in Cult Suicide Suggest Comet Was Sign to Die', Frank Bruni, 'Leader Believed in Space Aliens and Apocalypse', Gustav Niebuhr, 'On the Furthest Fringes of Millennialism', Heaven's Gate, 'Looking Forward to Trip Going to the Next Level', 'Statements That Heaven's Gate Released over the Years', *New York Times*, 28 March 1997, pp. A1, A11, A12; Todd S. Purdom, 'In Serene Setting in California, Eerie Scene Out of Hollywood', Gustav Niebuhr, 'Land of Religious Freedom Has Universe of Spirituality', David Gelernter, 'A Religion of Special Effects', *New York Times*, 30 March 1997, pp. A1, A14, A15, E11; R. Drummond Ayres, Jr., 'Cult Members Wrote a Script to Put Their Life and Times on the Big Screen', *New York Times*, 1 April 1997, p. A13; Barry Bearak, 'Eyes on Glory: Pied Pipers of Heaven's Gate', *New York Times*, 28 April 1997, pp. A1, A10–12. All quotes otherwise unidentified are from Heaven's Gate. The film reference is *Heaven's Gate*, dir. Michael Cimino (United Artists, 1980).

**82** Kathy Sawyer, 'Mars Probe Faces the Cold Truth', *International Herald Tribune*, 30 October 1997, p. 1; 'So Long Pathfinder', *Washington Post* editorial in *International Herald Tribune*, 31 October 1997, p. 8.

**83** 'So Long Pathfinder', 31 October 1997, p. 8.

# Credits

**INDEPENDENCE DAY**

**USA**

1996

**Production Companies**

Twentieth Century Fox presents a Centropolis Entertainment production

A Roland Emmerich film

**Director**

Roland Emmerich

**Executive Producers**

Roland Emmerich

Ute Emmerich

William Fay

**Producer**

Dean Devlin

**Associate Producer**

Peter Winther

**Production Supervisor**

New York:

Jane Nerlinger Evans

**Production Co-ordinators**

Dana Williams

New York:

Lonnie Kandel

Washington D.C.:

Alison Sherman

**Unit Production Managers**

Kelly Van Horn

New York:

William Fay

Location Managers

Supervisor:

Kenneth E. Fix

New York:

Jacob F. Conrad

Washington D.C.:

Peggy Pridemore

**2nd Unit Director**

Dean Devlin

**Aerial 2nd Unit Director/Co-ordinator**

Kevin Larosa

**Assistant Directors**

1st:

Sergio Mimica-Gezzan

2nd:

Kim H. Winther

2nd 2nd:

Michael Viglietta

Additonal 2nd:

Shari Hanger

2nd - New York:

Glen Trotiner

2nd 2nd - New York:

Dean Garvin

**Script Supervisors**

Susan Bierbaum

2nd Unit:

Annie Welles

Marvel Wakefield

**Casting**

Wendy Kurtzman

New York:

Bernard Telsey

Will Cantler

Associate:

Sharon Jetton

**Screenplay**

Dean Devlin

Roland Emmerich

**Director of Photography**

Karl Walter Lindenlaub

**Additional Photography**

Ueli Steiger

**Aerial Cameraman**

Kurt Soderling

**Aerial Assistant**

Steve Sass

**2nd Unit Director of Photography**

Jonathan Taylor

**Camera Operators**

Peter Joachim Krause

New York:

Bruce MacCallum, Tony C. Jannelli

**"B"Camera/Steadicam Operator**

Randy Nolen

**Steadicam Operator**

New York:

Rick Raphael

**Visual Effects**

Supervisors:

Volker Engel, Douglas Smith

Producer:

Terry Clotiaux

Production Office Co-ordinator:

Benedicte Naudin

Project Managers:

Marc Weigert

Nikolaus Kraemer

Editor:

Peter S. Elliot

Additional Editor:

Mark Eggenweiler

Camera Unit Production Supervisor:

Bob Hurrie

Co-ordinator:

Mark David Katchur

Directors of Photography:

Anna Foerster

Philipp Timme

High Speed Cam Op:

Jeff Sturgill

Motion Control Op:
Stephen Lebed
VFX Motion Controls
Prod Supervisors:
Carrie Owens
Lisa Knaggs
Prod Co-ordinators:
Joan Schneider
Yolie Moreno
Camera Operators:
Harry J. Alpert
James Balsam

**Minature Pyrotechnics/Special Effects Foreman:**
Emmet Kane

**Model Departments**
Shop Supervisor:
Michael Joyce
Art Director:
Steven Legler
Co-ordinator:
Maureen Reggie
Modelmakers:
David B. Beasley
Kento Gebo
Tom Griep
Eric Heisler
Jason "Kimba" Kaufman
Gil Koesters
Kenneth A. Larson
Brian Marn
Thomas Rush
Dennis "Buckwheat" Schultz
Paul Skylar
Greg Stuhl
Dave Ferris Emery
Bryson H. Gerard
John H. Hess
Tim Hutchausen
Mark Joyce
Thorsten Kohlmann
James D. Mcgeachy

Donald F. Matheson iii
Thorsten Schrecke
Christopher Simmons
Richard King Slifka
Robert H. Williams
Sculptors:
Jeff Frost
Steven Pinney
David Tye
Michael Hosch
Tully Summers
Eric Verderame

**Mechanical Effects**
1st Unit Supervisor:
Hans Metz
2nd Unit Supervisor:
Mike Edmonson
Technicians:
John S. Baker
Gary Bierend
Bill Greene
Nick Karas
Joshua R. Pinney
Martin Simon
Jeff Berrington
Al Broussard
Christopher Jones
D. Mike Paris
Matthew Pope
Mark Yuricich

**Digital Visual Effects**
Producer:
Steven T. Puri
Supervisors:
Tara Handy turner
Joseph Francis
Optical Sup:
Greg Kimble

**Comp Graphics Units**
Animation Sup:
Hartmut Engel
Animation Artists:
Kirk Cadrette
Steffan Herrmann

Benedikt Niemann
Jurgen "J.R." Schopper
Stephane Couture
Arthur Jeppe
Carolin Quis
Steffen M. Wild
Digital Compositor:
Conny Fauser-rumelin
Dig FX Prod Coords:
Peter Northbourne james
Rachele Troffer
Dig Matte Painter:
Michael Lloyd

**Digital Visual Effects Facilities**
Pacific Ocean Post Digital Film Group
Pacific Oceans
Executive Producers:
Allan Kozlowski
Jeff Ross
Digital VFX Producers:
Andrea D'amico
Stan Szymanski
Production Executive:
Scott Mcgrail
Digital Compositing Sup:
Pablo Helman
Digital Compositors:
Kenneth Littleton
Simon Haslett
Lawrence Littleton
Donna Tracy
Scott Rader
Jennifer German
John Rauh
Michael Peterson
Production Supervisor:
Dale Brodt
Editorial Co-ordinator:
Christopher Johnston
Production Co-ordinator:
Joe Stokes

**Digital Visual Effects Facilities**
Visionart Design and Animation
Digital Producer:
Joshua D. Rose
Digital Co-ordinator:
Richard J. Cook
Technical Supervisor:
Rob Bredow
CG Animators:
Daniel Kramer
Carl Hooper
Toan-Vinh Le
Pete Shinners
Todd Boyce
Digital Compositors:
Bethany Berndt-shackelford
Dorene Haver

**Digital Visual Effects Facility**
Digiscope
Executive Effects Producer:
Thomas Thill
Effects Producer:
Mary Stuart-welch
Digital Imaging Supervisor:
Dion Hatch
Digital Prod Supervisor:
Lorraine 'Deedle' Silver
Supervising Digital Artist:
Mitchell S. Drain
Digital Artist:
Marc Scott

**Digital Visual Effects Facility**
Post Group
Visual Effects Executive:
Mark Franco
Compositing Supervisor:
Peter Sternlicht
Digital Compositors:
Tom Smith Sr.

Steven J. Scott
Marty Rosenstock
Visual Effects Co-ordinator:
Karen Skouras
Digital Data Co-ordinator:
Linda Cordella

**Digital Visual Effects**
OCS/Freeze Frame/Pixel Magic
Digital VFX Supervisor:
Ray Mcintyre Jr.
Digital VFX Producer:
Philip O'Hanlon

**Additional Matte Painting**
Matte World Digital

**Creature Shop**
Patrick Tatopoulos Designs

**Mechanical Effects Supervisor**
Clay Pinney

**Alien Attacker Supervision**
Frank Bollinger

**Special Effects**
New York:
Steve Kirshoff

**Digital Effects Producer/Supervisor**
Tricia Ashford

**Miniature Pyrotechnics/Mechanical Fx Supervisor**
Joseph Viskocil

**Puppeteers**
Jake Garber
Fred Folger
Guy Himber
Gino Acevedo
Thomas Floutz

**Editor**
David Brenner

**Production Designers**
Oliver Scholl
Patrick Tatopoulos

**Art Department Co-ordinator**
Oana Bogdan
**Art Directors**
Jim Teegarden
New York:
Bonnie Brinkley
**Set Designers**
Pamela Klamer
Sean Haworth
Mick Cukurs
Julia Levine
**Set Decorator**
Jim Erickson
**Illustrators**
Tom Lay
Richard Buoen
Joseph F. Griffith Jr.
**Storyboard Artists**
Peter "Taco" Ramsey
Jacques Reisdorfer Rey
Rick Newsome
Jack Johnson
Trevor Goring
**Sculptor**
Dale B. Gordon
**Costume Designer**
Joseph Porro
**Costume Supervisors**
Riki Lin Sabusawa
New York:
Michael Adkins
Heidi Shulman
**Set Costumer**
Christi K. Work
**Costumes**
Estella C. Wallerstein
Irene A. Stepic
Rani Cunningham
**Make-up**
Zoltan
Katalin Elek
Michael F. Blake
Craig Smith

New York:
Lynn Campbell
**Alien Creature Effects**
**Design/Supervision**
Patrick Tatopoulos
**Hairstylists**
Joy Zapata
New York:
Aaron F. Quarles
**Main Titles**
Greenberg/Schluter
Visionart Design and
Animation
**Music**
David Arnold
**Music Orchestrator/**
**Conductor**
Nicholas Dodd
**Music Editors**
Supervisor:
Laurie Higgins Tobias
Additional:
Daniel Gaber
Doug Lackey
**Scoring Mixer**
Dennis Sands
**Songs**
'It's the End of the World As
We Know It' by William
Berry, Peter Buck,
Michael Mills, Michael Stipe,
performed by R.E.M.;
'Rumble' by Link Wray,
Milton Grant, performed by
Link Wray;
'Oh Vicki' by/performed by
Bill Elliott;
'About You' by Paul
Plaggent, Josh Gordon, Kyle
Baer, performed by Greta;
'Boom Boom Booty' by
Richard Rudolph, Michael
Sembello, Romany Malco,
performed by U.P.F., Rom;

'Stand By' by Sophie
Edkvist, Lars Halapi,
performed by Sophie
Zelmani;
'Live it Cool' by Junior
Vasquez, Lydia Rhodes,
performed by Lydia Rhodes
**Dance Sequence**
**Choreographer**
Anita Dawn Camp
**Sound Designer**
John Paul Fasal
**Sound Design/Editorial**
Jonathan Miller
Jon Johnson
**Sound Mixers**
Jeff Wexler
2nd Unit:
Bruce Bisenz
Mark Scheret
New York:
Tod A. Maitland
**Sound Recording**
Bob Renga
Craig "Pup" Heath
**Additional Recording**
Jim Bolt
Patrick Cyccone Jr.
Christian P. Minkler
Mike Casper
Dan Leahy
Sergio Reyes
B. Tennyson Sebastian III
**Re-recording Mixers**
Chris Carpenter
Bill W. Benton
Bob Beemer
**Supervising Sound**
**Editors**
Sandy Gendler
Val Kuklowsky
**Sound Editors**
Noah Blough
David M. Cowan

Steffan Falesitch
Scott G.G. Haller
Mark A. Lanza
Mark L. Mangino
John O. Wilde
Michael Chandler
Ronald Eng
Hector C. Gika
Nils Jensen
Mark R. La Pointe
William Van Daalen
Anthony Zero
**Sound Effects Recordists**
Ken Johnson
Eric Potter
**ADR**
Mixers:
Dean Drabin
J.R. Westen
Editors:
Gail Clark Burch
William Voigtlander
Uncle J. Kamen
C.T. Welch
Group Co-ordinator:
Burton Sharp
**Foley**
Artists:
John Roesch
Hilda Hodges
Supervising Editor:
Victor Radulich
Editors:
Vincent Cassaro
Nicholas James
**Satellite/Computer**
**Technical Adviser**
Chris Weaver
**Military Technical Adviser**
Dustin Salem
**Stunt Co-ordinator**
Dan Bradley
**Animals Provided by**
Di Sesso's Animals

**Pilots**
Ron Garlick
M. Evan Jensen
David R. Patrick
Rick Shuster
Dirk Vahle
Wayne F. Richardson
Henry Urgoiti
Ken Vieira

**Will Smith**
Captain Steven Hiller
**Bill Pullman**
President Thomas J.
Whitmore
**Jeff Goldblum**
David Levinson
**Mary McDonnell**
Marilyn Whitmore
**Judd Hirsch**
Julius Levinson
**Margaret Colin**
Constance Spano
**Randy Quaid**
Russell Casse
**Robert Loggia**
General William Grey
**James Rebhorn**
Albert Nimziki
**Harvey Fierstein**
Marty Gilbert
**Adam Baldwin**
Major Mitchell
**Brent Spiner**
Dr Brakish Okun
**James Duval**
Miguel
**Vivica A. Fox**
Jasmine Dubrow
**Lisa Jakub**
Alicia
**Ross Bagley**
Dylan

**Mae Whitman**
Patricia Whitmore
**Bill Smitrovich**
Captain Watson
**Kiersten Warren**
Tiffany
**Harry Connick Jr.**
Captain Jimmy Wilder
**Giuseppe Andrews**
Troy
**John Storey**
Doctor Isaacs
**Frank Novak**
Teddy
**Devon Gummersall**
Philip
**Leland Orser**
techy/medical assistant 1
**Mirron E. Willis**
**Ross Lacy**
aides
**David Pressman**
Whitmore's aide
**Vivian Palermo**
technician/medical
assistant
**Raphael Sbarge**
commander/technician
**Bobby Hosea**
**Dan Lauria**
commanding officers
**Steve Giannelli**
**Eric Paskel**
radar technicians
**Carlos Lacamara**
radar operator
**John Bennett Perry**
**Troy Willis**
secret servicemen
**Tim Kelleher**
technician
**Wayne Wilderson**
Area 51 technician

**Jay Acovone**
Area 51 guard
**James Wong**
SETI technician 1
**Thom Barry**
SETI technician 2
**Jana Marie Hupp**
SETI technician 3
**Matt Pashkow**
2nd officer
**Robert Pine**
chief of staff
**Marisa Morell**
co-worker 2
**Michael Winther**
co-worker 3
**Dexter Warren**
co-worker 4
**Paul Le Clair**
co-worker 5
**Captain Michael 'Chewy'
Vacca**
Lieutenant Peterson
**David Chanel**
secret service agent
**John Capodice**
Mario
**Greg Collins**
military aide
**Derek Webster**
sky crane pilot
**Mark Fite**
**Eric Neal Newman**
pilots
Levani
**Kristof Konrad**
Russian pilots
**Kevin Sifuentes**
tank commander
**Elston Ridgle**
soldier
**Randy Oglesby**
**Jack Moore**
mechanics

**Barry Del Sherman**
street preacher
**Lyman Ward**
secret service guy
**Anthony Crivello**
Lincoln
**Richard Speight Jr.**
Ed
**Barbara Beck**
Monica Soloway
**Joe Fowler**
**Andrew Warne**
**Sharon Tay**
reporters
**Peter Jozef Lucas**
Russian reporter
**Yelena Danova**
Russian newscaster
**Derek Kim**
Korean newscaster
**Vanessa J. Wells**
newscaster
**Jessika Cardinahl**
German video newscaster
**Gary W. Cruz**
**Ron Pitts**
**Wendy L. Walsh**
**Christine Devine**
**Mark Thompson**
video newscasters
**Ernie Anastos**
Rex Black, NY newscaster
**Kevin Cooney**
Atlantic Air CNC
**Rance Howard**
chaplain
**Nelson Mashita**
Japanese technician
**Jeff Phillips**
B-2 pilot
**Sayed Badreya**
Arab pilot
**Adam Tomei**

sailor
**John Bradley**
Lucas
**Kimberly Beck**
housewife
**Thomas F. Duffy**
lieutenant
**Andrew Keegan**
older boy
**Jon Matthews**
Thomson
**Jim Piddock**
Reginald
**Fred Barnes**
himself
**Eleanor Clift**
herself
**Jerry Dunphy**
Jack Germond
**Morton Kondracke**
John McLaughlin
**Barry Nolan**
**George Putnam**
themselves
**Eric Michael Zee**
Northridge field reporter
**Pat Skipper**
redneck
**Carlos Lara**
farmer kid
**Mike Monteleone**
Butler
**Lee Strauss**
Elvis fanatic
**Lisa Star**
woman on roof
**Malcolm Danare**
intellectual on roof
**Arthur Brooks**
trucker on roof
**Michael G. Moertl**
thief
**James J. Joyce**

master C.P.O.
**Joyce Cohen**
Kim Peters, reporter
**Julie Moran**
Entertainment Tonight
reporter
**Robin Groth**
Flagstaff news anchor
**Richard Pachorek**
LAPD helicopter pilot
**Dakota**
Boomer
**Gary Hecker**
alien vocal effects
**Frank Welker**
special vocal effects

13,105 feet
145 minutes

**Dolby**
**Colour by DeLuxe**
Super 35

**BFI Film Classics '... could scarcely be improved upon ... informative, intelligent, jargon-free companions.'**
The Observer

Each book in the BFI Publishing Film Classics series honours a great film from the history of world cinema. With new titles published each year, the series is rapidly building into a collection representing some of the best writing on film. If you would like to receive further information about future Film Classics or about other books on film, media and popular culture from BFI Publishing, please fill in your name and address and return this card to the BFI*.

No stamp is needed if posted in the UK, Channel Islands, or Isle of Man.

NAME

ADDRESS

POSTCODE

*North America: Please return your card to:
Indiana University Press, Attn: LPB, 601 N Morton Street,
Bloomington, IN 47401-3797

**BFI Publishing**
**21 Stephen Street**
**FREEPOST 7**
**LONDON**
**W1E 4AN**